Canadian Living's Best

Fish and Seafood

BY

Elizabeth Baird

AND

The Food Writers of Canadian Living® Magazine
and The Canadian Living Test Kitchen

A MADISON PRESS BOOK

PRODUCED FOR

BALLANTINE BOOKS AND CANADIAN LIVING

Ballantine Books	Canadian Living
A Division of	Telemedia
Random House of	Communications Inc.
Canada Limited	25 Sheppard Avenue West
2775 Matheson Blvd East	Suite 100
Mississauga, Ontario	North York, Ontario
Canada	Canada
L4W 4P7	M2N 6S7

Canadian Cataloguing in Publication Data

Baird, Elizabeth
Fish and seafood

(Canadian Living's best)
"Produced for Ballantine Books and Canadian Living."
Includes index.

ISBN 0-345-39872-6

1. Cookery (Fish). 2. Cookery (Seafood). I. Title. II. Series.

TX747.B34 1998   641.6'92   C98-931337-9

EDITORIAL DIRECTOR: Hugh Brewster
PROJECT EDITOR: Wanda Nowakowska
EDITORIAL ASSISTANCE: Beverley Renahan, Rosemary Hillary
PRODUCTION DIRECTOR: Susan Barrable
PRODUCTION COORDINATOR: Donna Chong
BOOK DESIGN AND LAYOUT: Gordon Sibley Design Inc.
COLOR SEPARATION: Colour Technologies
PRINTING AND BINDING: Imprimeries Transcontinental Inc.

CANADIAN LIVING ADVISORY BOARD: Elizabeth Baird, Bonnie Baker Cowan,
Anna Hobbs, Caren King

CANADIAN LIVING'S BEST FISH AND SEAFOOD
was produced by Madison Press Books
which is under the direction of Albert E. Cummings

Madison Press Books
40 Madison Avenue
Toronto, Ontario, Canada
M5R 2S1

Printed in Canada

Contents

Glazed Fish Fillets (p. 41)

Linguine with Clams and Tomatoes (p. 59)

Qualicum Chowder (p. 64)

Introduction

If there's one food that's right in step with today's health-conscious and busy lifestyle, it's fish and seafood. As nutritious as it is delicious, this bounty from our oceans, rivers and lakes comes in an amazing variety — from the humble and inexpensive species (the smelts, herrings, haddock, sardines, shark, catfish, mussels and mackerels) to the kingpins of the watery world (the oysters, shrimp, crab, salmon, char, trout, scallops, lobsters, halibut and swordfish) that we serve up for special occasions.

Adding to the multitude of choices are the forms in which fish and seafood present themselves to the interested cook — from dependable canned goods (think what lunch would be without salmon and tuna) to the products you can count on tucked in the freezer (the sole, cod and pollock fillets) and the glistening fish iced and waiting for takers at the fresh fish counter. Salting and smoking have also given fish exciting new tastes and textures.

But it's not just the variety and convenience of fish that appeal to today's busy cooks. It's the speed with which it goes from freezer, package or can to table, for deliciously easy meals any day of the week. Fish is naturally tender — its muscles consist of segments of rather short fibers, with significantly less connective tissue than meat and poultry. The result? A short cooking time — with less time spent getting the kinds of meals on the table that everyone enjoys, in the variety of tastes you can expect from *Canadian Living's* fine Test Kitchen and food writers.

Consider *Canadian Living's Best Fish and Seafood* a source of inspiration for your kind of cooking — fast, healthful, vibrantly flavored and suited to all occasions, from the all-important weeknight quickie to any kind of weekend entertaining.

Elizabeth Baird

Shrimp and Couscous Pilaf (p. 11)

Simmers and Quick-Fries

Cooked stovetop, seafood is extra-quick to make —
whether you steam or simmer it in broth, flip it in a hot skillet
or combine it with a potful of vegetables and rice.

Pan-Braised Sea Bass with Vegetables ▶

Here's a stylish dish that's perfect for weekend entertaining. Salmon is a colorful alternative; halibut, while not as vivid, is just as delicious.

Per serving: about
- 245 calories
- 9 g fat
- good source of iron
- 24 g protein
- 16 g carbohydrate

2	small leeks	2
1 tbsp	olive oil	15 mL
4	sea bass fillets (1 lb/500 g)	4
8	small carrots	8
1 cup	halved mushrooms	250 mL
1/2 tsp	dried thyme	2 mL
1/2 cup	chicken stock	125 mL
1/2 cup	dry white wine or chicken stock	125 mL
1	bay leaf	1
1 tsp	all-purpose flour	5 mL
1 tbsp	butter, softened	15 mL
Half	sweet red pepper, diced	Half
1/4 tsp	each salt and pepper	1 mL
2 tbsp	chopped fresh parsley	25 mL

● Remove root ends and all dark green parts from leeks. Slice white parts in half lengthwise; set aside.

● In large nonstick skillet, heat oil over medium-high heat; cook fillets for about 2 minutes per side or until browned. Transfer to plate.

● Add leeks, carrots, mushrooms and thyme to skillet; cook over medium heat, stirring, for about 5 minutes or until mushrooms begin to brown.

● Stir in chicken stock, wine and bay leaf; bring to boil. Reduce heat, cover and simmer for about 10 minutes or just until carrots are tender-crisp.

● In small bowl, blend flour with butter. Push vegetables to side of skillet. Stir butter mixture into liquid in skillet until smooth.

● Return fish to pan along with red pepper; simmer for about 15 minutes or just until fish is opaque and flakes easily when tested with fork. Discard bay leaf. Sprinkle with salt and pepper. Serve sprinkled with parsley. Makes 4 servings.

Dinner-Party Paella ◀

8 oz	chorizo sausage	250 g
1-3/4 lb	chicken legs	875 g
1 tbsp	olive oil	15 mL
1/4 tsp	saffron threads	1 mL
3 cups	warm chicken stock	750 mL
1	onion, chopped	1
2	cloves garlic, minced	2
1	can (28 oz/796 mL) tomatoes	1
1	small sweet green pepper, diced	1
1-1/2 cups	short-grain rice	375 mL
1/2 tsp	each salt and pepper	2 mL
1/2 cup	frozen peas	125 mL
12 oz	mussels	375 g
12 oz	large raw shrimp, peeled and deveined	375 g
2	green onions, minced	2
8	lemon wedges	8

● Cut sausage into 1/2-inch (1 cm) thick slices. Remove skin from chicken; trim off fat and cut at joint to separate thigh from drumstick. In large paella pan or deep wide skillet, heat oil over high heat; cook sausage for about 2 minutes or until browned. Remove to plate. Reduce heat to medium; cook chicken for 7 to 10 minutes per side or until browned. Add to plate.

● Stir saffron into chicken stock; set aside to soften. Add onion and garlic to pan; cook, stirring, for 4 minutes or until softened. Add stock mixture, tomatoes and green pepper; bring to boil, breaking up tomatoes with back of spoon and scraping up any brown bits from bottom of pan. Stir in rice, salt and pepper; reduce heat to low. Add chicken; simmer gently, stirring often, for 20 minutes. Gently stir in peas and sausage.

● Meanwhile, scrub mussels under running water; trim off beards. Discard any that do not close when tapped. Nestle mussels and shrimp in rice until almost covered; cook for 7 to 10 minutes or until rice is tender, shrimp are pink and mussels are open. Discard any mussels that do not open. Garnish with onions and lemon. Makes 8 servings.

*P*aella's colorful selection of sweet peppers, green peas, seafood, chicken and chorizo sausage gives it enormous "wow" appeal as a party dish. Garnish with trimmed fresh artichoke brushed with lemon juice to prevent browning.

Per serving: about
- 443 calories
- 17 g fat
- good source of iron
- 32 g protein
- 40 g carbohydrate

TIP: You can use clams instead of mussels, or replace chorizo with any spicy sausage.

Shrimp in Black Bean Sauce

1-1/2 cups	long-grain rice	375 mL
2 tbsp	vegetable oil	25 mL
4	cloves garlic, minced	4
1 tbsp	chopped shallots or minced gingerroot	15 mL
1 lb	large raw shrimp, peeled and deveined	500 g
1/3 cup	dry white wine	75 mL
2 tbsp	(approx) black bean sauce	25 mL

● In saucepan, bring 3 cups (750 mL) water to boil; stir in rice. Reduce heat, cover and simmer for 15 to 20 minutes or until rice is tender and liquid is absorbed.

● Meanwhile, in skillet, heat oil over medium-high heat; cook garlic and shallots, stirring, for 1 minute. Add shrimp; cook, stirring, for about 2 minutes or until pink and opaque.

● Add wine and black bean sauce, adding up to 1 tbsp (15 mL) more sauce to taste. Bring to boil; cook for 1 minute. To serve, spoon shrimp over rice. Makes 4 servings.

*H*ere's how to bring home the flavors of a popular Chinese restaurant dish. The secret is black bean sauce made from fermented black soybeans. The sauce is a convenience Chinese product like hoisin or oyster sauce, all available in most supermarkets.

Per serving: about
- 435 calories
- 9 g fat
- good source of iron
- 23 g protein
- 60 g carbohydrate

Risotto from the Sea

Risotto may sound complicated, but it's just as easy to make as a soup. Here's a basic one with cod, but other mild fish will work well, too.

Per serving: about
- 500 calories
- 26 g protein
- 23 g fat
- 46 g carbohydrate
- good source of iron

8 oz	cod fillets	250 g
1/4 cup	butter	50 mL
2 tbsp	olive or vegetable oil	25 mL
1	onion, chopped	1
4 cups	(approx) chicken stock	1 L
1-1/3 cups	short-grain rice (preferably Arborio)	325 mL
1 cup	frozen peas	250 mL
1/4 cup	chopped fresh parsley	50 mL
1/4 cup	freshly grated Parmesan cheese	50 mL
	Salt and pepper	

● Pat fillets dry; cut into 1-1/2-inch (4 cm) pieces. Set aside.

● In large saucepan, melt half of the butter with the oil over medium heat; cook onion, stirring occasionally, for about 5 minutes or until golden. Meanwhile, in small saucepan, heat chicken stock until hot; keep hot over very low heat.

● Add rice to onion; cook, stirring constantly, for about 5 minutes or until edges of grains are translucent. Pour in 1/2 cup (125 mL) hot stock; reduce heat and simmer, stirring constantly, for about 5 minutes or until most of the liquid is absorbed.

● Repeat with enough of the remaining stock, adding in 1/2 cup (125 mL) additions and cooking for about 25 minutes in total, or until rice is just tender and mixture is still creamy.

● Add fish to rice mixture; cover and simmer for 2 minutes or until fish is opaque. Rinse peas with hot water; gently stir into rice mixture along with parsley, cheese, remaining butter, and salt and pepper to taste. Makes 4 servings.

Shrimp Sausage Gumbo

A burnished roux — flour and oil cooked over low heat until deep butterscotch in colour — is at the heart of Cajun cooking. So is heat and spiciness. Since an authentic hot Cajun sausage is hard to find up north, try this delicious gumbo with a peppery Italian or Portuguese sausage.

Per each of 8 servings: about
- 345 calories
- 22 g protein
- 21 g fat
- 16 g carbohydrate
- good source of iron

1/4 cup	vegetable oil	50 mL
1/2 cup	all-purpose flour	125 mL
4	cloves garlic, minced	4
4	stalks celery, chopped	4
3	onions, chopped	3
1 tsp	pepper	5 mL
1/2 tsp	each cayenne pepper, dried thyme and oregano	2 mL
2	bay leaves	2
6 cups	chicken stock	1.5 L
1 lb	spicy smoked sausage, sliced	500 g
1	each sweet red and green pepper, chopped	1
1 lb	raw shrimp, peeled and deveined	500 g

● In large heavy skillet, cook oil with flour over low heat, stirring almost constantly, for about 30 minutes or until butterscotch color.

● Add garlic, celery, onions, pepper, cayenne, thyme, oregano and bay leaves; cook over medium-high heat, stirring, for 3 minutes. Gradually whisk in stock. Add sausage; bring to boil. Reduce heat and simmer for 1 hour or until liquid is thickened.

● Add red and green peppers; cook for 15 minutes. Add shrimp; simmer for 5 minutes or until pink. Discard bay leaves. Makes 6 to 8 servings.

TIP: Because the sausage and chicken stock are salty, serve this gumbo on unsalted rice.

Shrimp and Couscous Pilaf ▲

1 tbsp	vegetable oil	15 mL
2	cloves garlic, minced	2
1	onion, chopped	1
2	zucchini, chopped	2
1-1/4 tsp	curry powder	6 mL
1/4 tsp	each salt and pepper	1 mL
12 oz	frozen cooked shrimp, thawed	375 g
1-1/2 cups	couscous	375 mL
1	apple, chopped	1
1/3 cup	raisins	75 mL
2 cups	chicken stock	500 mL
1/4 cup	plain yogurt (optional)	50 mL

● In heavy saucepan, heat oil over medium heat; cook garlic, onion, zucchini, curry powder, salt and pepper, stirring occasionally, for about 5 minutes or until onion is softened.

● Add shrimp, couscous, apple and raisins; stir to coat. Pour in stock; bring to boil, stirring often. Remove from heat; cover and let stand for 5 minutes. Fluff with fork. Serve dolloped with yogurt (if using). Makes 4 servings.

Couscous looks like a grain but it's really a form of coarsely ground hard wheat called semolina. Like instant rice, it has been precooked and rehydrates to a fluffy failproof pilaf in just five minutes.

Per serving: about
- 490 calories
- 6 g fat
- very high source of fiber
- 30 g protein
- 78 g carbohydrate
- excellent source of iron

TIP: Bulk food stores are a good place to introduce yourself to a new product such as couscous. You can buy as much as you wish, and the bulk price is usually less than the packaged.

Boiled Lobster

Tuck a napkin around your neck and enjoy lobster the classic way — steaming hot and ready for dipping in melted butter. Atlantic breezes are optional, but very nice!

Per serving: about
- 172 calories
- 1 g fat
- 36 g protein
- 2 g carbohydrate

Dipping Sauce, per tbsp (15 mL): about
- 22 calories
- 2 g fat
- 1 g protein
- 1 g carbohydrate

4	live lobsters (each 1-1/2 lb/750 g)	4
1/2 cup	butter, melted, or Lemon Chive Dipping Sauce (recipe follows)	125 mL

● Fill large deep pot with enough salted water (1 tbsp/15 mL salt per 4 cups/1 L water) to completely cover lobsters; bring to full rolling boil over high heat. With tongs, grasp back of each lobster; plunge headfirst into water. Cover and return to boil.

● Start cooking time when water boils; reduce to bubbly simmer. Cook each lobster for 10 minutes for first pound (500 g) and 1 minute for each additional 4 oz (125 g) or until lobster is bright red and small leg comes away easily when twisted and pulled. Immediately remove from water.

● Remove meat from lobster as follows, discarding shells and setting meat aside or dipping into butter to eat as you proceed.

● First, twist off claws at joint at body; separate into claw and arm sections. Break off smaller part of claw and remove meat with lobster pick or nut pick. Using lobster cracker or nutcracker, crack larger part of claw at widest part; lift out meat. Crack arm; pick out meat.

● Separate tail piece from body by twisting apart. Bend tail backward and break off flippers; pick out meat from each flipper.

● Using kitchen shears or steak knife, cut through shell along underside of tail to expose meat. With fingers or fork, pry meat from shell. Remove and discard intestinal vein (if any).

● Holding legs and inner section of body, pull off back shell. Remove and eat red coral (if any) and green tomalley (liver). Insert thumbs in inner section of body and pry apart to separate in half lengthwise; extract any meaty tidbits. Break off legs; suck out juice and meat. Makes 4 servings.

LEMON CHIVE DIPPING SAUCE		
1/2 cup	low-fat plain yogurt	125 mL
1/4 cup	light mayonnaise	50 mL
4 tsp	chopped fresh chives or green onion	20 mL
1 tbsp	lemon juice	15 mL
1 tsp	Dijon mustard	5 mL
Pinch	cayenne pepper	Pinch

● In small bowl, stir together yogurt, mayonnaise, chives, lemon juice, mustard and cayenne pepper. Makes 3/4 cup (175 mL).

COOKING AND EATING LOBSTER
● For even cooking, buy lobsters of similar weight. Cook 1-1/4 lb (625 g) lobsters for 11 to 13 minutes; 1-1/2 lb (750 g) for 12 to 14 minutes; 1-3/4 lb (875 g) for 13 to 15 minutes.
● If you don't have lobster crackers, use kitchen shears to cut along edge of claws. If you don't have any picks, use small fork to remove meat.

Lean Fish with Salsa for One ▲

4 cups	packed fresh spinach (about 5 oz/150 g)	1 L
3 oz	cod fillet	90 g
1 tbsp	lime juice	15 mL
Pinch	each salt and pepper	Pinch
	SALSA	
1 tbsp	lime juice	15 mL
1	small clove garlic, minced	1
1-1/2 tsp	granulated sugar	7 mL
Dash	hot pepper sauce	Dash
1/4 cup	diced peeled mango	50 mL
1 tbsp	finely chopped red onion	15 mL
Half	sweet red pepper, diced	Half

● SALSA: In bowl, mix together lime juice, garlic, sugar and hot pepper sauce. Add mango, onion and red pepper; toss to coat.

● Trim and rinse spinach; shake off excess water and arrange spinach, with just the water clinging to leaves, over bottom of small nonstick skillet. Top with fillet; sprinkle with lime juice, salt and pepper.

● Cover and steam for 2 to 3 minutes or until fish is opaque and flakes easily when tested with fork. Serve with salsa. Makes 1 serving.

*I*nstead of picking up light frozen entrées, try this satisfying single-serving supper with fresh ingredients from the produce and fish counters.

Per serving: about
- 185 calories
- 1 g fat
- very high source of fiber
- excellent source of iron
- 20 g protein
- 26 g carbohydrate
- good source of calcium

Tomato Dill Trout for One ▲

This colorful fish entrée can be cooked to perfection in the microwave — or try baking or barbecuing it, for a change. It's simple to multiply ingredients for more servings.

Per serving: about
- 195 calories
- 6 g fat
- good source of iron
- 25 g protein
- 10 g carbohydrate

1/4 cup	chopped onion	50 mL
1/4 cup	diced sweet red or green pepper	50 mL
Half	tomato, seeded and chopped	Half
1/4 cup	sliced mushrooms	50 mL
1/2 tsp	olive oil	2 mL
Half	small clove garlic, minced	Half
1/4 tsp	each salt and pepper	1 mL
1 tbsp	chopped fresh dill	15 mL
4 oz	trout fillets, skinned	125 g
1 tsp	lime or lemon juice	5 mL

● In 2-cup (500 mL) microwaveable casserole dish, mix together onion, red pepper, tomato, mushrooms, oil, garlic and half each of the salt and pepper; cover and microwave at High for 2 minutes.

● Stir in half of the dill; top with fillets. Sprinkle with lime juice and remaining dill, salt and pepper. Cover and microwave at High for 2 minutes. Let stand for 5 minutes. Makes 1 serving.

● TO BAKE: Bake vegetable mixture, covered, in 400°F (200°C) oven or toaster oven for 10 minutes. Add remaining ingredients; bake, covered, for 10 minutes or until fish is opaque and flakes easily when tested with fork.

● TO BARBECUE: Center vegetable mixture on large square of heavy-duty foil. Top with remaining ingredients. Fold foil over and seal with double fold; tuck ends under. Place on grill over medium-high heat; cook for 20 minutes, turning once.

Smoked Black Cod

4	smoked black cod fillets (1 lb/500 g)	4
Pinch	pepper	Pinch
	HERB HORSERADISH SAUCE	
1/4 cup	tarragon vinegar or white wine vinegar	50 mL
1	shallot, sliced (or 1/4 cup/50 mL sliced onion)	1
1	small clove garlic, sliced	1
1/4 tsp	pepper	1 mL
1/2 cup	white wine	125 mL
2	each sprigs fresh thyme and tarragon	2
2	egg yolks	2
1 tsp	horseradish	5 mL
1/3 cup	butter, at room temperature	75 mL
1 tbsp	each chopped fresh chives and parsley	15 mL

● HERB HORSERADISH SAUCE: In small saucepan, bring vinegar, shallot, garlic and pepper to boil; boil for 3 minutes or until reduced to half. Add wine, thyme and tarragon; boil for 3 minutes or until reduced to half. Strain into measure to make about 1/4 cup (50 mL); let cool.

● In heatproof bowl over saucepan of hot (not boiling) water, whisk together egg yolks, horseradish and vinegar mixture; cook, whisking constantly, for about 5 minutes or until paler, thickened to consistency of whipping cream and hot to the touch. Strain into bowl; whisk in butter until melted. Stir in chives and parsley.

● Meanwhile, sprinkle fillets with pepper; place in single layer in skillet and cover with cold water. Cover tightly and bring to simmer over medium heat; simmer for 8 minutes. Transfer to paper towels; pat dry. Place on plates; drizzle with sauce. Makes 4 servings.

From Bishop's Restaurant in Vancouver comes this tasty dish — smoky, dense fish perfectly mated to a rich sauce that's spiked with horseradish. A little different, and very delicious! The sauce is also tasty with salmon or roasted halibut.

Per serving: about
- 282 calories
- 22 g protein
- 19 g fat
- 2 g carbohydrate

Haddock with Light Cream Sauce

1 cup	fish or chicken stock	250 mL
1	onion, minced	1
1 lb	haddock fillets	500 g
1/4 tsp	pepper	1 mL
1/4 cup	light cream cheese, cubed	50 mL
1 tbsp	each chopped fresh dill and chives	15 mL

● In skillet, bring stock, 1/4 cup (50 mL) water and onion to boil; reduce heat, cover and simmer for 5 minutes.

● Arrange fillets over onion mixture; season with pepper. Cover and steam, basting twice, for 5 to 7 minutes or until fish is opaque and flakes easily when tested with fork. With slotted lifter, transfer fish to plates; keep warm.

● Boil liquid in skillet for 2 minutes; stir in cheese, whisking until thickened and smooth, about 2 minutes. Spoon over fish. Sprinkle with dill and chives. Makes 4 servings.

Melting cream cheese into poaching liquid makes a quick, creamy sauce. If you have a bottle of dry white wine open, pour 1/2 cup (125 mL) into the poaching pan along with 1/2 cup (125 mL) fish stock.

Per serving: about
- 150 calories
- 24 g protein
- 5 g fat
- 2 g carbohydrate

TIP: Boiled new potatoes tossed with parsley can't be beat as the starch to go along with quick-cooking fish fillets.

STEAMERS

Common steamers are made of bamboo, steel or aluminum. Bamboo ones with lids are designed to sit in a wok that is at least 3 inches (8 cm) larger in diameter. Metal ones often come with their own shallow pots for water. If space is a concern, look for round bamboo or metal racks that fit into your wok. In a pinch, a small cake rack will do. Or set two wooden chopsticks a few inches apart in your wok, then balance a platter on them. A dome-shaped lid allows steam to circulate. If you don't have a large enough wok, substitute a roasting pan with a rack and a lid.

Steamed Whole Rockfish ▼

A whole fish, signifying abundance, is a must at Chinese New Year, and Vancouver chef/author Stephen Wong recommends rockfish, a West Coast specialty. You can also try this recipe with any fish small enough to fit into a wok or steamer — including snapper, trout or whitefish, or even fish fillets or steaks.

Per serving: about
- 165 calories
- 5 g fat
- 27 g protein
- 1 g carbohydrate

1-1/2 lb	rockfish (with head and tail), cleaned and scaled	750 g
2 tsp	coarse sea salt	10 mL
4	green onions	4
2 tbsp	dry sherry	25 mL
1/4 cup	shredded gingerroot	50 mL
2 tbsp	chicken stock	25 mL
2 tbsp	soy sauce	25 mL
1 tbsp	sesame oil	15 mL
	Fresh coriander sprigs (optional)	

● Rub outside and cavity of fish with salt; let stand for 10 minutes. Rinse off salt; pat dry.

● Place steam rack or steamer in wok; pour in enough water to come 1 inch (2.5 cm) below rack. Cover and bring to boil over medium-high heat.

● Using broad side of heavy knife, smash 2 of the onions; cut each in half crosswise. Place on heatproof platter that will fit in wok. Place fish on onions; pour sherry evenly over top. Sprinkle with ginger.

● Place plate on rack; steam for 8 to 10 minutes or until fish is opaque and flakes easily when tested with fork. Transfer to serving platter, discarding onions and juices.

● Meanwhile, cut remaining onions into matchstick-size pieces. In small saucepan, bring chicken stock, soy sauce and oil just to boil. Sprinkle onions over fish; pour boiling stock mixture evenly over top. Garnish with coriander (if using). Makes 4 servings.

TIP: Did you know that the ginger and sherry combination is a classic Chinese way to get rid of fish odors and strong flavors?

Steamed Fillets with Herb Vinaigrette

1 lb	thick fish fillets	500 g
3 tbsp	red wine vinegar	50 mL
3 tbsp	rice vinegar	50 mL
2 tbsp	finely chopped red onion	25 mL
1 tbsp	chopped fresh dill	15 mL
1 tsp	capers	5 mL
1 tsp	each chopped fresh basil and chives	5 mL
1/4 tsp	each salt and pepper	1 mL
1/4 cup	olive oil	50 mL

● In steamer set over boiling water, cover and steam fillets for 5 to 10 minutes or until fish is opaque and flakes easily when tested with fork.

● Meanwhile, in blender, purée together red wine vinegar, rice vinegar, onion, dill, capers, basil, chives, salt and pepper; with machine running, slowly pour in oil. Serve drizzled over fish. Makes 4 servings.

A pristine steamed fish fillet, drizzled with fresh herbs in a tangy oil and vinegar dressing, is both a pretty sight and a delicious repast.

Per serving: about
- 249 calories
- 24 g protein
- 16 g fat
- 2 g carbohydrate

Pickerel with Creamy Sauce

1/4 cup	all-purpose flour	50 mL
2 tbsp	chopped fresh dill (or 1 tsp/5 mL dried dillweed)	25 mL
Pinch	each salt and pepper	Pinch
2	pickerel fillets (unskinned), about 1-1/2 lb (625 g)	2
2 tbsp	butter	25 mL
1/4 cup	lemon juice	50 mL
	Lemon Cream Sauce or Lemon Duxelles (recipes follow)	

● In shallow dish, mix together flour, dill, salt and pepper; gently press fillets into flour mixture, turning to coat and shaking off excess.

● In large skillet, melt butter over medium heat; cook fillets, skin side up, for 4 minutes. Turn and sprinkle with lemon juice; cook for about 3 minutes or until fish flakes easily when tested with fork. Serve with Lemon Cream Sauce or Lemon Duxelles. Makes 4 servings.

Amy's on Second restaurant in Prince Albert, Saskatchewan, invites guests to enjoy northern freshwater pickerel with either of these superb sauces.

Per serving (without sauce): about
- 195 calories
- 25 g protein
- 7 g fat
- 5 g carbohydrate

CREAMY SAUCES FOR PICKEREL

Lemon Cream Sauce

● In small saucepan, bring 1/2 cup (125 mL) whipping cream, 2 tbsp (25 mL) lemon juice and 1/2 tsp (2 mL) Worcestershire sauce to simmer over medium heat; cook, stirring occasionally, for about 7 minutes or until reduced to half and thickened enough to coat back of spoon. Makes 1/3 cup (75 mL).

Per tbsp (15 mL): about • 74 calories • 1 g protein • 8 g fat • 1 g carbohydrate

Lemon Duxelles

● In small saucepan, melt 1 tbsp (15 mL) butter over medium heat; cook 1 cup (250 mL) finely chopped mushrooms and 1/4 cup (50 mL) chopped onion, stirring occasionally, for about 5 minutes or until onion is softened. Add 1 minced clove garlic, 1/2 cup (125 mL) whipping cream, 1 tbsp (15 mL) lemon juice and pinch salt; cook, stirring occasionally, for about 5 minutes or until reduced to half and thickened enough to coat back of spoon. Makes 2/3 cup (150 mL).

Per tbsp (15 mL): about • 49 calories • trace protein • 5 g fat • 1 g carbohydrate

Rösti with Smoked Salmon

You can skip the line-ups at Toronto's popular Marché and Mövenpick restaurants and make your own delicious version of their signature dish — super-crisp potato pancakes topped with sour cream and smoked salmon.

Per serving: about
- 475 calories
- 32 g fat
- 14 g protein
- 34 g carbohydrate

2	baking potatoes (unpeeled)	2
1/4 tsp	salt	1 mL
Pinch	pepper	Pinch
2 tbsp	butter, melted	25 mL
2 tbsp	olive oil	25 mL
1/4 cup	sour cream	50 mL
4 oz	thinly sliced smoked salmon	125 g

● In saucepan of boiling salted water, cook potatoes for 15 minutes or just until tender. Drain and rinse in cold water; drain and refrigerate for at least 4 hours or for up to 8 hours.

● Peel and coarsely grate potatoes into bowl to make 2-1/2 cups (625 mL). Toss with salt and pepper. Combine butter with oil. In 7-inch (18 cm) skillet, heat 1 tbsp (15 mL) of the butter mixture over medium heat; spread half of the potatoes evenly in pan, pressing firmly. Cook for 8 minutes or until edges are golden. Invert large plate over skillet; flip rösti onto plate.

● Spread another 1 tbsp (15 mL) butter mixture over skillet; slide rösti back into pan, uncooked side down. Cook for 10 minutes or until golden on bottom. Remove to plate; keep warm. Repeat with remaining potato and butter mixture.

● Serve each rösti topped with sour cream and smoked salmon. Makes 2 servings.

Quick Curried Fillets

Mild fish fillets are like an unpainted canvas just waiting for cooks to be creative with their favorite flavors. Food writer and author Rose Murray has opted for curry here — with delicious results.

Per serving: about
- 250 calories
- 13 g fat
- 25 g protein
- 8 g carbohydrate

2 tbsp	butter	25 mL
1 tbsp	curry powder	15 mL
1/4 cup	finely chopped peeled apple	50 mL
1	small onion, chopped	1
1	clove garlic, minced	1
1 lb	fish fillets	500 g
1/2 cup	light sour cream	125 mL
1 tsp	cornstarch	5 mL
	Salt	
1/4 cup	coarsely chopped toasted cashews or peanuts	50 mL
2 tbsp	sliced green onions	25 mL

● In large skillet, melt butter over medium-low heat; blend in curry powder and cook, stirring, for about 1 minute or until fragrant. Add apple, onion and garlic; cook, stirring, for 2 minutes.

● Add fillets; cover and cook, turning once, for about 5 minutes or until fish is opaque and flakes easily when tested with fork. Transfer fish to serving platter; cover and keep warm.

● Combine sour cream with cornstarch and stir into pan; increase heat to medium and cook, stirring, for 2 to 3 minutes or until thickened and smooth. Season with salt to taste. Pour over fish; sprinkle with nuts and green onions. Makes 4 servings.

TIP: Toast cashews in heavy skillet over medium heat, stirring frequently, for 5 to 7 minutes or until golden.

Fish Cakes ▲

1	large baking potato	1
1 lb	fish fillets	500 g
1	egg, beaten	1
1/4 cup	minced green onion	50 mL
2 tbsp	minced fresh parsley	25 mL
1 tbsp	chopped fresh dill	15 mL
1 tbsp	light mayonnaise	15 mL
1/2 tsp	salt	2 mL
1/4 tsp	pepper	1 mL
Dash	hot pepper sauce	Dash
1/2 cup	fine dry bread crumbs	125 mL
2 tbsp	vegetable oil	25 mL

● Peel and quarter potato. In saucepan of boiling salted water, cook potato for 17 to 20 minutes or until tender. Remove with slotted spoon; drain and rice or mash.

● In same water, poach fillets over medium-low heat for 5 minutes or until fish flakes easily when tested with fork; drain and process in food processor until smooth.

● In bowl, combine potato, fish, egg, onions, parsley, dill, mayonnaise, salt, pepper and hot pepper sauce; form into 8 oval patties, 1/2 inch (1 cm) thick. In shallow dish, press patties into crumbs to coat all over; press one end into fish-tail shape.

● In large nonstick skillet, heat oil over medium-high heat; cook patties for 3 minutes. Using two spatulas, turn patties carefully; cook for 2 to 3 minutes longer or until golden brown. Makes 4 servings.

C*runchy cakes are a tasty way to serve fish, especially to the young crowd. Form into fantasy shapes with carrots and celery for eyes and mouth, or pat into rounds for quick suppers.*

Per serving: about
- 275 calories
- 11 g fat
- good source of iron
- 26 g protein
- 18 g carbohydrate

Pan-Fried Fillets with Mushrooms

Smother fillets with mushrooms and you've got an impressive main course in minutes. Serve with crunchy greens — broccoli is always a healthful choice — and a baked potato, regular or sweet.

Per serving: about
- 210 calories
- 23 g protein
- 11 g fat
- 5 g carbohydrate

2 tbsp	all-purpose flour	25 mL
3/4 tsp	salt	4 mL
1/2 tsp	dried tarragon	2 mL
1/4 tsp	pepper	1 mL
1 lb	flounder fillets	500 g
2 tbsp	butter	25 mL
2 cups	sliced mushrooms	500 mL
2 tbsp	chopped fresh parsley	25 mL
1 tbsp	lemon juice	15 mL
1 tbsp	vegetable oil	15 mL

● In shallow dish, combine flour, salt, tarragon and pepper. Press fillets into mixture to coat all over. Set aside.

● In skillet, melt half of the butter over medium heat; cook mushrooms, stirring often, for 6 to 8 minutes or until golden. Remove with slotted spoon to bowl; toss with parsley and lemon juice. Set aside.

● Add remaining butter and oil to skillet; cook fish over medium-high heat for 3 minutes; turn and top with mushroom mixture. Cook for 3 to 4 minutes or until fish is golden brown outside, opaque inside and flakes easily when tested with fork. Makes 4 servings.

Cornmeal-Crusted Fish

Fennel, oregano and basil bring the flavors of Italy to the table. Vary the herbs in this master coating mix depending on what your family likes and what you have on hand.

Per serving: about
- 160 calories
- 20 g protein
- 5 g fat
- 9 g carbohydrate

1/4 cup	cornmeal	50 mL
1 tbsp	all-purpose flour	15 mL
2 tsp	dried oregano	10 mL
1-1/2 tsp	dried basil	7 mL
1/2 tsp	fennel seeds, crushed	2 mL
1/4 tsp	each salt and pepper	1 mL
4	fish fillets (1 lb/500 g)	4
1 tbsp	vegetable oil	15 mL

● In shallow dish, combine cornmeal, flour, oregano, basil, fennel seeds, salt and pepper. Press fillets into mixture to coat all over.

● In skillet, heat oil over medium-high heat; cook fillets, turning once, for about 5 minutes or until fish is opaque and flakes easily when tested with fork. Makes 4 servings.

Crispy-Fried Pickerel

When deep-frying, be sure to use only fresh oil and exercise extra care with this cooking method.

Per serving: about
- 339 calories
- 33 g protein
- 12 g fat
- 22 g carbohydrate
- good source of calcium and iron

1/4 cup	all-purpose flour	50 mL
1/4 cup	milk	50 mL
1	egg	1
2 cups	saltine cracker crumbs	500 mL
2 lb	pickerel fillets, skinned	1 kg
	Vegetable oil	
	Salt	

● Place flour in shallow bowl. In separate shallow bowl, whisk milk with egg. Place cracker crumbs in another shallow bowl.

● Cut fillets diagonally into 2-inch (5 cm) wide pieces. In deep-fryer, heat oil to 375°F (190°C). Meanwhile, dip fish, one piece at a time, into flour, shaking off excess, then into milk mixture, then into cracker crumbs, turning and pressing to coat all over.

● Fry fish, a few pieces at a time, for 3 to 4 minutes or until golden and fish rises to top of fryer. Transfer to paper towel-lined platter; sprinkle with salt to taste. Makes 6 servings.

Ten-Minute Trout with Lime

1-1/2 lb	salmon trout fillets or thin salmon fillets (with skin)	750 g
1 tsp	dried thyme	5 mL
1/4 tsp	each salt and pepper	1 mL
1 tbsp	butter	15 mL
4	green onions, sliced	4
1	lime or lemon, cut in wedges	1

● Sprinkle flesh side of fillets with thyme, salt and pepper. In large nonstick skillet, melt butter over medium-high heat; cook fish, skin side up, for about 4 minutes or just until bottom is nicely browned.

● Turn fish over and sprinkle with onions; cook for about 2 minutes or until fish is opaque and flakes easily when tested with fork. Serve with lime to squeeze over top. Makes 4 servings.

Skillet-bronzed fish accented with a squeeze of lime is an amazing main course you can whip up in just ten minutes.

Per serving: about
- 255 calories
- 13 g fat
- 31 g protein
- 2 g carbohydrate

TIP: If you can't find salmon trout, the thin tail piece of a salmon fillet will substitute nicely. Other alternatives are red snapper, haddock, sole, turbot, pollock (Boston bluefish) or orange roughy.

Haddock with Peach and Pepper Salsa

1 lb	haddock fillets	500 g
1	egg	1
1 cup	dry bread crumbs	250 mL
1/4 tsp	each salt and pepper	1 mL
2 tsp	butter	10 mL
	PEACH AND PEPPER SALSA	
1/2 cup	diced peeled fresh peach	125 mL
1/2 cup	diced sweet red pepper	125 mL
1/4 cup	diced onion	50 mL
1 tbsp	chopped fresh coriander or parsley	15 mL
1 tbsp	lime juice	15 mL
1/4 tsp	hot pepper sauce	1 mL

● PEACH AND PEPPER SALSA: In small bowl, combine peach, red pepper, onion, coriander, lime juice and hot pepper sauce; cover and refrigerate for up to 2 hours.

● Cut haddock into 4 pieces if necessary, removing any bones. In shallow dish, lightly beat egg. In another shallow dish, combine bread crumbs, salt and pepper. Gently press fillets into crumb mixture, turning to coat and shaking off excess.

● In large skillet, melt butter over medium heat; cook fillets, turning once, for about 8 minutes or until fish flakes easily when tested with fork. Serve garnished with salsa. Makes 4 servings.

Lean, mild haddock tops the list when maritimers choose fish. This dish, with its colorful mosaic of seasonal produce, is featured at Bluenose Lodge in Lunenburg, Nova Scotia.

Per serving: about
- 253 calories
- 5 g fat
- 27 g protein
- 23 g carbohydrate

FISH FILLETS

● When buying fresh fillets, choose glistening, translucent, firm ones with no fishy odor. Frozen fillets are sold in packages of solid blocks, portion sizes or individual fillets.

● When pan-frying, baking, broiling or roasting fish, most fillets are interchangeable, and it's only a question of adjusting times for the thinner fillets such as flounder and sole.

● When barbecuing, choose thick fillets and opt for firm-fleshed fish, such as monkfish, Boston bluefish, salmon steaks or fillets, sea bass, rainbow trout, halibut and grouper.

Easy Bakes

There's no tastier invitation to dinner than deliciously crisp fish straight from the oven — you can almost taste the golden crunchy edges and steaming moist flakes.

Oven-Baked Fish and Chips ▶

Indulge in a family favorite without all the fat and soggy newspaper that come with store-bought. Baking the fillets at extra-high heat is the secret to lower-fat flavor. A tasty cornflake coating adds the crispness and crunch.

Per serving: about
- 390 calories
- 29 g protein
- 10 g fat
- 46 g carbohydrate
- excellent source of iron

3	baking potatoes	3
2 tbsp	vegetable oil	25 mL
3/4 tsp	each salt and pepper	4 mL
3 cups	corn flakes	750 mL
1/4 cup	all-purpose flour	50 mL
1 tsp	dried Italian herb seasoning	5 mL
1 tsp	grated lemon rind	5 mL
1	egg	1
1 tbsp	milk	15 mL
4	halibut or cod fillets (1 lb/500 g)	4

● Scrub potatoes; cut each into 8 wedges. Toss with oil and 1/4 tsp (1 mL) each of the salt and pepper; place on large rimmed baking sheet. Bake in 450°F (230°C) oven for 20 minutes. Turn and bake for 10 minutes longer or until crisp and golden outside and tender inside; move to edge of baking sheet.

● Meanwhile, pour corn flakes into plastic bag. Using rolling pin, crush to make coarse crumbs; transfer to plate. On separate plate, stir together flour, herb seasoning, lemon rind and remaining salt and pepper.

● In shallow dish, whisk egg with milk. Dip each fillet into flour mixture, shaking off excess. Dip into egg mixture, then into crumbs, pressing lightly to coat. Place in center of baking sheet. Return to oven for about 8 minutes or until fish is crispy and flakes easily when tested with fork. Makes 4 servings.

FISH IS GREAT FOR YOUR HEALTH!
The Heart and Stroke Foundation of Canada recommends eating fish two or three times a week.

● Fish is high in protein and is also a source of iron and B vitamins. Lean fish such as sole, cod and haddock has as little as 1 g fat per serving. Higher-fat fish such as salmon, mackerel, trout, tuna, herring and swordfish contains essential heart-healthy omega-3 fatty acids.

● Omega-3 fatty acids are a type of polyunsaturated fat found in the tissues of sea creatures. These crucial nutrients have been linked to lower blood pressure, may lower blood triglycerides (a high level is a risk factor in the development of heart disease) and may reduce blood stickiness which, in turn, reduces clotting.

Chili Cheese Fish Stacks ▼

Alberta journalist Joanne Good is celebrated for her 6 o'clock survival suppers. Here's one that always goes over well in her household. She serves it with tomato slices, green beans, rice and salsa.

Per serving: about
- 498 calories
- 35 g protein
- 29 g fat
- 23 g carbohydrate
- good source of iron

1-1/2 lb	fish fillets	750 g
4 oz	herbed cream cheese	125 g
1	can (114 mL) diced green chilies, drained	1
1 cup	fine dry bread crumbs	250 mL
1 tsp	chili powder	5 mL
1	egg	1
1 tbsp	water or milk	15 mL

● Cut fillets into 8 equal pieces. Top half with slivers of cream cheese; press chilies into cheese. Top with remaining fish.

● In shallow dish, mix bread crumbs with chili powder. In another shallow dish, beat egg with water. Holding each stack together, dip into egg mixture, then into crumbs, turning to coat.

● Place fish on greased baking sheet and bake in 450°F (230°C) oven, turning halfway through, for 8 to 10 minutes or until fish is opaque and flakes easily when tested with fork.
Makes 4 servings.

Parmesan Baked Fillets

1 cup	light mayonnaise	250 mL
1/2 cup	finely chopped fresh parsley	125 mL
1/4 tsp	dried thyme	1 mL
1/2 cup	dry bread crumbs	125 mL
1/2 cup	freshly grated Parmesan cheese	125 mL
1 lb	fish fillets	500 g

● Stir together mayonnaise, parsley and thyme. In shallow dish, mix bread crumbs with cheese. Pat fillets dry with paper towels.

● Spread mayonnaise mixture on both sides of fillets. Dip each into crumb mixture, turning to coat; place on greased baking sheet.

● Bake in 450°F (230°C) oven for 8 to 10 minutes or until fish is opaque and flakes easily when tested with fork. Makes 4 servings.

Light mayonnaise provides the glue that holds crumbs and cheese on tasty fillets.

Per serving: about
- 390 calories
- 24 g fat
- good source of calcium
- 28 g protein
- 14 g carbohydrate

Busy-Night Lemon-Baked Fish

1/2 tsp	grated lemon rind	2 mL
1 tbsp	lemon juice	15 mL
1 tbsp	vegetable oil	15 mL
2	cloves garlic, minced	2
1 lb	fish fillets	500 g
	Salt and pepper	

● Stir together lemon rind and juice, oil and garlic.

● OVEN METHOD: Arrange fillets in shallow baking dish; sprinkle with salt and pepper to taste. Spread lemon mixture over fish. Bake in 450°F (230°C) oven for 8 to 10 minutes or until fish is opaque and flakes easily when tested with fork.

● MICROWAVE METHOD: Arrange fillets in round microwaveable dish with thickest part toward outside; sprinkle with salt and pepper to taste. Spread lemon mixture over fish. Cover with waxed paper; microwave at High for 4 to 6 minutes or until fish is opaque and flakes easily when tested with fork. Let stand, covered, for 5 minutes. Makes 4 servings.

Ten minutes is all you need to cook this lemon-accented fish dish. Keep a package of your favorite frozen fillets handy in the freezer for this quick recipe.

Per serving: about
- 120 calories
- 4 g fat
- 19 g protein
- 1 g carbohydrate

NO INSTRUCTIONS REQUIRED

Too busy to look up a recipe for a quick dinner? Fish, quickly cooked and well accompanied by so many different flavors, is the ideal solution to the suppertime blues. Try these recipe-free ideas for a fast-fix meal.

● Bake in foil or parchment paper with thinly sliced red onion, thinly sliced lemon or lime and a dollop of prepared pesto.

● Serve broiled or grilled with your favorite salsa.
● Brush with your favorite prepared salad dressing before broiling or grilling.

● Brush with hoisin or teriyaki sauce or your favorite Asian glaze before cooking.
● Brush with sweet mustard thinned with a little oil before cooking.

● Marinate in yogurt stirred with a little curry paste. Grill and serve with sliced cucumber.

Peanut Crunch Fillets ▲

A *peanut and bread crumb coating, clinging to fillets with beaten egg, crisps in the dry heat of the oven and keeps the fillets moist inside.*

Per serving about
- 380 calories
- 18 g fat
- good source of iron
- 33 g protein
- 21 g carbohydrate

1 cup	fine dry bread crumbs	250 mL
1/2 cup	finely chopped peanuts	125 mL
1/2 tsp	salt	2 mL
1/4 tsp	pepper	1 mL
2	eggs, beaten	2
4 tsp	vegetable oil	20 mL
1 lb	fish fillets	500 g

● In shallow dish, combine bread crumbs, peanuts, salt and pepper. In small bowl, beat eggs with oil. Pat fillets dry with paper towels.

● Dip each fillet into egg mixture, then into crumb mixture, turning to coat; place on greased baking sheet. *(Fish can be prepared to this point, covered and refrigerated for up to 6 hours.)*

● Bake in 450°F (230°C) oven for 6 minutes. Turn and bake for 1 to 3 minutes longer or until crispy and fish is opaque and flakes easily when tested with fork. Makes 4 servings.

Lemon Pepper Roasted Cod

1 lb	thick cod fillet	500 g
2 tbsp	light mayonnaise	25 mL
2 tsp	grated lemon rind	10 mL
1/4 tsp	coarsely ground pepper	1 mL
1/4 cup	sliced almonds	50 mL

● Place fillet on greased rack on rimmed baking sheet. Combine mayonnaise, lemon rind and pepper; spread over fish. Bake in 450°F (230°C) oven for 7 minutes.

● Sprinkle with nuts; bake for 5 minutes or until nuts are golden and fish is opaque and flakes easily when tested with fork. Makes 4 servings.

Haddock is a good substitute when cod is not available.

Per serving: about
- 150 calories
- 21 g protein
- 6 g fat
- 2 g carbohydrate

Pizza-Style Fish Fillets

1 lb	fish fillets	500 g
1/2 cup	tomato sauce	125 mL
1/4 cup	diced sweet green pepper	50 mL
1/4 cup	minced fresh parsley	50 mL
1/2 tsp	dried basil	2 mL
1/4 tsp	dried marjoram	1 mL
1 cup	shredded mozzarella cheese	250 mL
	Freshly grated Parmesan cheese	

● Arrange fillets in greased 13- x 9-inch (3.5 L) baking dish. Spoon tomato sauce on top; sprinkle with green pepper, parsley, basil, marjoram, then mozzarella.

● Bake in 450°F (230°C) oven for 6 to 10 minutes or until bubbly and fish is opaque and flakes easily when tested with fork. Sprinkle with Parmesan cheese to taste. Makes 4 servings.

Convert junior fish fraidies to fish lovers by presenting fillets à la pizza — with tomato sauce, green peppers and mozzarella toppings. Add other favorite pizza choices, if you like.

Per serving: about
- 195 calories
- 28 g protein
- 7 g fat
- 4 g carbohydrate
- good source of calcium

Arctic Char with Shrimp

1/3 cup	butter	75 mL
1	onion, chopped	1
2	stalks celery, chopped	2
4 cups	fresh bread crumbs	1 L
2 tbsp	chopped fresh parsley	25 mL
2 tbsp	chopped fresh dill	25 mL
2	green onions, chopped	2
1 tsp	salt	5 mL
1/2 tsp	pepper	2 mL
1 lb	frozen cooked baby shrimp, thawed	500 g
5 lb	Arctic char or salmon, deboned and cleaned	2.2 kg
	Salt and pepper	

● In skillet, melt butter over medium heat; cook onion and celery, stirring occasionally, for 5 to 8 minutes or until softened. Remove from heat. Stir in bread crumbs, parsley, dill, green onions, salt, pepper and shrimp.

● Pat fish cavity dry; sprinkle cavity with salt and pepper to taste. Fill cavity with stuffing; sew or skewer closed. Bake on greased baking sheet in 425°F (220°C) oven for 45 to 55 minutes or until flesh is opaque and flakes easily when tested with fork. Makes 8 servings.

From food writer Bonnie Stern comes this memorable stuffing for one of Canada's finest fish. Ask your fish monger to remove the bones while keeping the skin and flesh of the char intact.

Per serving: about
- 458 calories
- 33 g protein
- 17 g fat
- 42 g carbohydrate
- good source of iron

Lemon-Roasted Salmon ▶

Welcome to the easy way to entertain — with a whole roasted salmon. The availability of farm-raised salmon has made this majestic fish much more affordable, too.

Per serving: about
- 242 calories
- 15 g fat
- 23 g protein
- 2 g carbohydrate

1	salmon, cleaned (5 lb/2.2 kg)	1
1/4 tsp	each salt and pepper	1 mL
3	lemons, sliced	3
1/2 cup	each fresh dill and parsley sprigs	125 mL
2 tbsp	butter, melted	25 mL
	CREAMY DILL WINE SAUCE	
2 tbsp	butter	25 mL
2 tbsp	all-purpose flour	25 mL
1/2 cup	each milk, dry white wine and whipping cream	125 mL
3/4 tsp	salt	4 mL
1/4 tsp	pepper	1 mL
1/4 cup	chopped fresh dill	50 mL

● Using sharp knife, firmly cut off fish head behind gills (or have fishmonger remove it). Rinse under cold water; pat dry. Season inside and out with salt and pepper. Arrange one-third of the lemon slices in lengthwise row along center of foil-lined rimmed baking sheet; top with salmon.

● Fill cavity with dill, parsley and another third of the lemons. Brush butter over salmon; top with remaining lemons. Crumple up foil around fish to hold juices, leaving salmon uncovered.

● Bake salmon in 450°F (230°C) oven for about 45 minutes, or 10 minutes per inch (2.5 cm) of thickness, or until flesh is opaque and flakes easily when tested with fork. Remove from oven and tent with foil; let stand for 5 minutes. With baster or spoon, remove 1/4 cup (50 mL) pan juices; set aside.

● CREAMY DILL WINE SAUCE: In saucepan, melt butter over medium heat; stir in flour and cook, stirring, for 1 minute. Gradually whisk in milk, wine, cream, salt and pepper; cook, whisking, for 5 minutes or until boiling and thickened. Stir in reserved pan juices; reduce heat and simmer for 5 minutes. Keep warm over low heat while carving salmon; stir in dill.

● To serve salmon, discard lemon on top. Cut lengthwise along backbone through to bone. Starting at backbone, gently pull off skin; discard. Cut along midline, parallel to backbone, through to bone. Cut crosswise into 4-inch (10 cm) wide portions. Inserting spatula between meat and bones, lift salmon portions to warmed serving plates.

● Gently lift exposed bones away from other side of salmon; discard. Repeat cutting along midline, then into portions; ease salmon away from skin. Serve with warm sauce. Makes 12 servings.

FRESH IS BEST

Here's how to choose the freshest of fresh fish and seafood.

● Reputable fish markets and supermarkets with an active turnover are the best places to buy fish and seafood. Don't ever be afraid to ask what's the freshest and to adjust your menu accordingly.
● Fish fillets and steaks should be moist with no dried-out or discolored edges, have an iridescent pearly look and be elastic enough to spring back when touched.
● Whole fish should be firm, with bright red gills, clear protruding eyes and scales that adhere tightly.

● No fresh fish or seafood ever smells fishy. Make your choice on a mild, almost sweet fragrance, with a clean ocean scent coming from ocean species.
● Plan on eating fresh fish the day of purchase. If you must keep it for the next day, cover fish lightly with plastic wrap and store in coldest part of the refrigerator.
● Cover mussels, clams and oysters with damp towels and refrigerate for as brief a time as possible, no longer than one day.

Roasted Salmon with Wild Rice

This recipe has its origins at Vancouver's Granville Market, where five species of Pacific salmon are sold during the summer spawning season.

Per each of 10 servings: about
- 287 calories
- 25 g protein
- 14 g fat
- 15 g carbohydrate

1 cup	wild rice, rinsed	250 mL
1 tsp	(approx) salt	5 mL
2 tbsp	butter	25 mL
1 cup	finely chopped mushrooms	250 mL
1/2 cup	finely chopped onion	125 mL
1	clove garlic, minced	1
1/2 cup	slivered almonds or pine nuts	125 mL
1 tsp	crumbled dried thyme	5 mL
1/2 tsp	crumbled dried sage	2 mL
1/4 tsp	pepper	1 mL
2 tbsp	lemon juice	25 mL
1	salmon, cleaned (4 to 5 lb/2 to 2.2 kg)	1
1 tbsp	butter, melted	15 mL
	Watercress	
2	lemons, cut in wedges	2

● In saucepan, combine 2 cups (500 mL) water, rice and 1/2 tsp (2 mL) of the salt; cover and bring to boil. Reduce heat and simmer for 25 to 30 minutes or until rice is tender but not mushy. If necessary, uncover and cook briefly just until no moisture remains. Spread on baking sheet and let cool; transfer to bowl.

● Meanwhile, in large skillet, melt butter over medium heat; cook mushrooms, onion, garlic, almonds, thyme, sage, pepper and pinch of salt, stirring occasionally, until onion is softened and nuts slightly browned. Mix into rice along with 1 tbsp (15 mL) of the lemon juice.

● Wipe salmon inside and out with damp cloth. Brush cavity with remaining lemon juice; sprinkle with remaining 1/2 tsp (2 mL) salt. Fill with stuffing. Place any leftover stuffing in heatproof dish and cover. Sew or skewer cavity closed.

● Place fish on lightly greased rimmed baking sheet; brush with melted butter. Bake in 450°F (230°C) oven for 10 minutes per inch (2.5 cm) of thickness or until flesh is opaque and flakes easily when tested with fork. Bake any extra stuffing along with fish.

● Let fish stand for 5 minutes. Transfer to heated platter; carefully remove string and skin from top side of salmon. Garnish with watercress and lemon wedges. Arrange extra stuffing around cavity opening. Makes 8 to 10 servings.

Spicy Roasted Swordfish

High-heat roasting mellows the spices and concentrates the flavors. Note the other kinds of fish that taste good with this Cajun-inspired coating.

Per serving: about
- 215 calories
- 34 g protein
- 7 g fat
- 2 g carbohydrate
- good source of iron

1 tbsp	lime or lemon juice	15 mL
1-1/2 tsp	chili powder	7 mL
1 tsp	each paprika, pepper, dried oregano and dried thyme	5 mL
1/4 tsp	each garlic powder and salt	1 mL
4	swordfish, halibut or salmon steaks (1-1/2 lb/750 g)	4

● In small bowl, whisk together lime juice, 2 tsp (10 mL) water, chili powder, paprika, pepper, oregano, thyme, garlic powder and salt; rub gently onto both sides of fish.

● Place fish on baking sheet; bake in 425°F (220°C) oven for about 10 minutes or until fish is opaque and flakes easily when tested with fork. Makes 4 servings.

TIP: Try shark steaks, too. This rub also works well with fillets as long as they are at least 3/4 inch (2 cm) thick. Choose monkfish, catfish, whitefish or snapper.

Baked Stuffed Whitefish

1/4 cup	butter	50 mL
1-1/2 cups	chopped mushrooms	375 mL
2	stalks celery, diced	2
1	onion, chopped	1
2 tbsp	chopped fresh parsley	25 mL
1 tbsp	chopped fresh sage (or 1 tsp/5 mL dried crushed)	15 mL
1/2 tsp	(approx) each salt and pepper	2 mL
1/2 tsp	ground ginger	2 mL
2 cups	coarse fresh bread crumbs	500 mL
1	whitefish, cleaned (about 2-1/2 lb/1.25 kg)	1
1 tbsp	vegetable oil	15 mL

● In large skillet, melt butter over medium heat; cook mushrooms, celery and onion, stirring occasionally, for 5 minutes or until softened.

● Stir in parsley, sage, salt, pepper and ginger; cook for 2 minutes. Remove from heat; stir in bread crumbs.

● Pat fish cavity dry; sprinkle cavity with salt and pepper to taste. Fill cavity loosely with stuffing; fasten with skewers. Place on greased rimmed baking sheet; brush with oil.

● Bake in 450°F (230°C) oven for 10 minutes per inch (2.5 cm) of thickness, about 25 minutes, or until flesh is opaque and flakes easily when tested with fork. Makes 4 servings.

O*wen Sound, Ontario, is on Georgian Bay where whitefish plucked out of its cold waters are sold at the weekly Saturday market. Baked whole, whitefish is tasty with an old-fashioned bread stuffing.*

Per serving: about
● 456 calories ● 38 g protein
● 26 g fat ● 16 g carbohydrate

Sauced Smoked Fish

1 lb	smoked cod fillets, cut in 4	500 g
2-1/2 cups	milk	625 mL
1/4 cup	butter	50 mL
1	small onion, chopped	1
2 tbsp	all-purpose flour	25 mL
Pinch	pepper	Pinch
	Chopped fresh parsley	
	Lemon slices	

● In large skillet, cover fillets with milk and bring to simmer over low heat; poach for 10 minutes. Transfer fish to 8-inch (2 L) square baking dish; strain poaching liquid, reserving 1-1/2 cups (375 mL).

● In saucepan, melt butter over medium heat; cook onion, stirring occasionally, for 3 minutes or until softened. Stir in flour; cook over low heat, stirring, for 3 minutes without browning.

● Whisk in reserved poaching liquid and pepper; cook, stirring, for 5 minutes or until thickened and smooth.

● Pour sauce over fish; bake in 350°F (180°C) oven for 15 minutes or until bubbly. Serve garnished with parsley and lemon. Makes 4 servings.

S*moked cod basks under a creamy oven-glazed blanket. The recipe is adapted from a breakfast specialty at Nova Scotia's Liscombe Lodge, where, by the way, one of the best breakfasts in Canada is served.*

Per serving: about
● 265 calories ● 24 g protein
● 14 g fat ● 9 g carbohydrate

Roasted Salmon with Tomatoes and Lentils

This popular French bistro dish is healthful, easy to prepare at home and, best of all, according to cooking school owner and author Bonnie Stern, "it's absolutely delicious."

Per serving: about
- 370 calories
- 34 g protein
- 11 g fat
- 36 g carbohydrate
- very high source of fiber
- excellent source of iron

1-1/2 cups	dried green lentils, rinsed	375 mL
4 tsp	olive oil	20 mL
1	onion, chopped	1
2	cloves garlic, minced	2
2 tsp	chopped fresh rosemary (or 1/4 tsp/1 mL dried)	10 mL
1 tsp	ground cumin	5 mL
1/4 tsp	hot pepper flakes	1 mL
1	each carrot and stalk celery, finely diced	1
2 cups	puréed canned tomatoes	500 mL
1/4 cup	chopped fresh parsley	50 mL
1 tsp	salt	5 mL
1/2 tsp	pepper	2 mL
1-1/2 lb	salmon fillet, skinned and cut in 6 pieces	750 g

● In saucepan, cover lentils generously with water; bring to boil. Reduce heat and simmer for 25 to 35 minutes or until lentils are tender. Drain well.

● Meanwhile, in large nonstick skillet, heat 1 tbsp (15 mL) of the oil over medium heat; cook onion and garlic, stirring occasionally, for about 5 minutes or until tender. Add 1 tsp (5 mL) of the rosemary, cumin and hot pepper flakes; cook for 30 seconds.

● Add carrot and 3 tbsp (50 mL) water; cook for 5 minutes. Add celery and tomatoes; cook for 10 minutes or until carrots are tender-crisp. Add lentils, parsley, salt and pepper. Keep warm.

● In nonstick ovenproof skillet, heat remaining oil over medium-high heat. Sprinkle salmon with remaining rosemary; place in skillet and cook for 1 to 2 minutes per side or until lightly browned and crusty.

● Transfer to 400°F (200°C) oven; bake for 7 to 9 minutes or until fish is opaque and flakes easily when tested with fork. Serve over lentil mixture. Makes 6 servings.

Tomato-Smothered Halibut

Brenda Humchitt, a member of the West Coast Heiltsuk band, often prepares fresh halibut dishes like this one for her family.

Per serving: about
- 184 calories
- 25 g protein
- 7 g fat
- 6 g carbohydrate

2 tbsp	butter	25 mL
2	onions, sliced	2
1-1/2 cups	canned plum tomatoes (including juice)	375 mL
1/2 tsp	each salt and pepper	2 mL
1-1/2 lb	halibut steaks	750 g
1 tbsp	chopped fresh basil	15 mL

● In heavy saucepan, melt butter over medium heat; cook onions, stirring occasionally, for about 10 minutes or until just beginning to brown. Stir in tomatoes and juice, breaking up with fork; sprinkle with half each of the salt and pepper. Cook for about 3 minutes or until slightly thickened.

● Meanwhile, cut halibut into 6 pieces, removing bones; sprinkle with remaining salt and pepper. Place in greased 13- x 9-inch (3 L) baking dish. Spoon tomato sauce over fish; sprinkle with basil. Bake in 450°F (230°C) oven for 10 to 15 minutes or until fish is opaque and flakes easily when tested with fork. Makes 6 servings.

Salmon with Roasted Vegetables ▼

2	onions	2
4	carrots	4
2	large zucchini	2
1	large sweet red pepper	1
1	can (14 oz/398 mL) artichoke hearts	1
2 tbsp	olive oil	25 mL
4	cloves garlic, minced	4
4	anchovies, chopped (or 1 tbsp/15 mL anchovy paste)	4
2 tsp	dried thyme	10 mL
3/4 tsp	each salt and pepper	4 mL
2 tbsp	white wine vinegar	25 mL
4	salmon fillets (with skin), 1 inch (2.5 cm) thick (6 oz/175 g each)	4

● Peel and cut onions in half lengthwise, leaving root end intact; cut each half into 4 wedges. Peel and cut carrots in half lengthwise; cut into chunks. Quarter zucchini lengthwise; cut into chunks. Core and seed red pepper; cut into chunks. Drain and quarter artichoke hearts.

● In large skillet, heat half of the oil over medium heat; cook onions, garlic, carrots, anchovies, 1-1/2 tsp (7 mL) of the thyme, and 1/2 tsp (2 mL) each of the salt and pepper, stirring often, for about 10 minutes or until vegetables are softened. Remove from heat.

● Stir in zucchini, red pepper, artichoke hearts and vinegar. Transfer vegetables to large rimmed baking sheet. Bake in 425°F (220°C) oven, stirring often, for about 25 minutes or until carrots and zucchini are tender-crisp.

● In small bowl, combine remaining oil, thyme, salt and pepper; brush over top of fillets. Place, skin side down, on vegetables. Bake for 10 to 15 minutes or until fish is opaque and flakes easily when tested with fork. Makes 4 servings.

This magnificent supper features the king of fish and showcases healthy vegetables as a colorful bed on which the succulent salmon is presented.

Per serving: about
- 420 calories
- 18 g fat
- very high source of fiber
- 37 g protein
- 30 g carbohydrate
- excellent source of iron

Grills and Broils

Summertime, and the grilling is easy and delicious — especially when seafood is the star of the deck or backyard barbecue.

Grill-Pan Salmon Steaks ▶

Get a great year-round barbecue taste and typical marks using a ridged cast-iron grill pan on your stove. Of course, you can barbecue these steaks outside, too.

Per serving: about
- 246 calories
- 13 g fat
- 29 g protein
- 2 g carbohydrate

2 tbsp	(approx) olive oil	25 mL
1 tbsp	vinegar	15 mL
1 tbsp	grated orange rind	15 mL
1/3 cup	orange juice	75 mL
2	cloves garlic, minced	2
2 tsp	paprika	10 mL
1/2 tsp	each salt and cayenne pepper	2 mL
4	salmon steaks or fillets (6 oz/175 g each)	4

● Whisk together oil, vinegar, orange rind and juice, garlic, paprika, salt and cayenne; set aside 2 tbsp (25 mL). Pour remainder into shallow glass dish; add salmon, turning to coat. Cover and marinate for 30 minutes, turning once.

● Heat grill pan over medium heat until pan sizzles when sprinkled with a few drops of water. Brush with oil. Grill salmon for about 4 minutes per side or just until opaque and fish flakes easily when tested with fork. To serve, brush with reserved marinade. Makes 4 servings.

Smoke-Grilled Salmon

You don't need a smoker to enhance fish with an authentic smoky flavor. Try this barbecue method of simultaneously cooking and smoking with other thick fish fillets, too.

Per serving: about
- 225 calories
- 10 g fat
- 30 g protein
- trace carbohydrate

1 tsp	grated lime rind	5 mL
1/4 cup	lime juice	50 mL
1 tbsp	vegetable oil	15 mL
1 tsp	Dijon mustard	5 mL
Pinch	pepper	Pinch
4	salmon steaks, 1 inch (2.5 cm) thick (1-1/2 lb/750 g)	4
1/3 cup	toasted sesame seeds (optional)	75 mL

● Whisk together lime rind and juice, oil, mustard and pepper; pour into shallow glass dish. Add salmon, turning to coat. Cover and marinate for 30 minutes, turning occasionally.

● Reserving marinade, remove fish; sprinkle with sesame seeds (if using). Place on greased grill over pan of soaked wood chips on medium heat. Close lid and cook, turning and basting with marinade halfway through, for 16 to 20 minutes or until fish is opaque and flakes easily when tested with fork. Makes 4 servings.

TIP: Soak wood chips in water for 30 minutes, chunks for 60; set in foil pan directly on coals.

Chili-Crusted Salmon Steaks ▲

M ayonnaise is the coating ingredient that glosses so beautifully when fish is roasted or broiled under high heat.

Per serving: about
- 270 calories
- 14 g fat
- 31 g protein
- 2 g carbohydrate

4	salmon steaks (1-1/2 lb/750 g)	4
1 tsp	vegetable oil	5 mL
Pinch	each salt and pepper	Pinch
3 tbsp	light mayonnaise	50 mL
1 tbsp	lime or lemon juice	15 mL
1	chipotle pepper, minced	1
2 tsp	adobo sauce	10 mL

● Place salmon in shallow glass dish; brush one side with oil. Sprinkle with salt and pepper; turn fish over.

● Stir together mayonnaise, lime juice, chipotle pepper and adobo sauce; spread evenly over top of fish. *(Salmon can be covered and refrigerated for up to 2 hours.)* Let stand at room temperature for 30 minutes.

● Place salmon, oil side down, on broiler rack or foil-lined baking sheet; broil for about 10 minutes or until golden and bubbly and fish flakes easily when tested with fork. Makes 4 servings.

CHIPOTLE PEPPERS

Look for chipotle peppers — roasted smoked jalapeño peppers — in cans in Mexican specialty stores or at the supermarket. The rich mahogany-red sauce in which the peppers are packed delivers just as much fire power as the peppers themselves.

● The standard-size can contains more peppers than can be used at one time, so it's a good idea to freeze leftovers. Pour the remaining peppers and sauce into a resealable freezer bag, gently pressing out air and separating peppers so that it will be easy to break off a section of pepper and sauce without thawing the whole package.

Smoky Salmon Barbecue

1/2 cup	chili sauce	125 mL
1/4 cup	vegetable oil	50 mL
1/4 cup	white wine vinegar	50 mL
2 tsp	Worcestershire sauce	10 mL
1 tsp	packed brown sugar	5 mL
1 tsp	hickory liquid smoke	5 mL
4	salmon steaks (1-1/2 lb/750 g)	4

● Whisk together chili sauce, oil, vinegar, Worcestershire sauce, sugar and liquid smoke; pour into shallow glass dish. Add salmon, turning to coat. Cover and marinate for 30 minutes, turning once.

● Reserving marinade, place salmon on greased grill over medium-high heat; close lid and cook, turning once and basting frequently with marinade, for 10 minutes per inch (2.5 cm) of thickness or until fish is opaque and flakes easily when tested with fork. Makes 4 servings.

This simple — and simply fabulous — coating marinade has starred at the annual Great Taste of British Columbia Salmon Barbecue.

Per serving: about
• 365 calories
• 22 g fat
• 31 g protein
• 10 g carbohydrate

Grilled Salmon Fillets

1 lb	salmon fillet (with skin)	500 g
	LEMON DILL MARINADE	
1/3 cup	olive oil	75 mL
1 tsp	grated lemon rind	5 mL
1/4 cup	lemon juice	50 mL
2 tbsp	chopped fresh dill (or 2 tsp/10 mL dried dillweed)	25 mL
1/4 tsp	each salt and pepper	1 mL

● LEMON DILL MARINADE: Whisk together oil, lemon rind and juice, dill, salt and pepper; pour into shallow glass dish.

● Cut fillet into 4 pieces, removing any bones with tweezers if necessary. Add to marinade, turning to coat. Cover and marinate for up to 30 minutes, turning occasionally.

● Reserving marinade, place fillets, skin side down, on greased grill over medium-high heat. Close lid and cook, turning halfway through, basting frequently and using all the marinade, for 10 minutes per inch (2.5 cm) of thickness or until fish is opaque and flakes easily when tested with fork. Makes 4 servings.

VARIATIONS

● TERIYAKI MARINADE: Marinate fish in mixture of 1/4 cup (50 mL) soy sauce, 4 tsp (20 mL) white wine vinegar, 2 tsp (10 mL) granulated sugar, 2 tsp (10 mL) vegetable oil and 1 clove garlic, minced.

● LIME CUMIN MARINADE: Marinate fish in mixture of 1/4 cup (50 mL) olive oil, 1/4 cup (50 mL) lime juice, 4 tsp (20 mL) Worcestershire sauce, 1-1/2 tsp (7 mL) ground cumin, 1 tsp (5 mL) grated lime rind, 2 cloves garlic, minced, and 1/4 tsp (1 mL) each salt and pepper.

For best results, choose thick fillets with the skin on to hold the flesh together while cooking.

Per serving: about
• 277 calories
• 21 g fat
• 21 g protein
• 1 g carbohydrate

TIP: Be sure to marinate fish no longer than specified; otherwise, it will "cook" in the acids of the marinade and become dry during grilling.

Asian Grilled Salmon ▲

Choose a thick, even center cut from a salmon fillet and let it soak up the Asian-flavored marinade before grilling it slowly over low heat.

Per serving: about
- 245 calories
- 13 g fat
- 28 g protein
- 3 g carbohydrate

2 lb	salmon fillet (with skin)	1 kg
2 tbsp	each vegetable oil, lemon juice and soy sauce	25 mL
1 tbsp	each packed brown sugar and minced gingerroot	15 mL
2	cloves garlic, minced	2
Pinch	each pepper and cayenne pepper	Pinch

● Make several shallow diagonal slashes in skinless side of salmon. Place, skin side up, in shallow glass dish.

● Whisk together oil, lemon juice, soy sauce, sugar, ginger, garlic, pepper and cayenne; pour over salmon. Cover and marinate for 30 minutes.

● Discarding marinade, place fillet, skin side down, on greased grill over low heat; close lid and cook for about 30 minutes or until fish is opaque and flakes easily when tested with fork. Makes 6 servings.

Cedar-Planked Salmon

1-1/2 lb	salmon fillet (with skin)	750 g
1/4 cup	olive oil	50 mL
2 tsp	grated lemon or orange rind	10 mL
1/4 cup	lemon or orange juice	50 mL
1 tbsp	chopped fresh basil	15 mL
1 tsp	pepper	5 mL
1/2 tsp	salt	2 mL

● Place salmon, skin side down, in large glass dish. Whisk together oil, lemon rind and juice, basil, pepper and salt; pour over salmon. Cover and refrigerate for at least 2 hours or for up to 8 hours.

● Discarding marinade, place salmon, skin side down, on soaked cedar plank. Place plank on grill over medium-high heat; close lid and cook for about 20 minutes or until fish is opaque, bronze-colored and flakes easily when tested with fork. Makes 6 servings.

For this traditional East Coast aboriginal way of cooking fish adapted to a modern barbecue, choose a cedar plank at your local lumberyard. Get one a little larger than the fish and soak it in cold water for at least four hours or overnight before using.

Per serving: about
- 175 calories
- 21 g protein
- 10 g fat
- 1 g carbohydrate

Broiled Fish with Parsley Chive Sauce

1/2 cup	dry bread crumbs	125 mL
Pinch	each salt and pepper	Pinch
1 lb	white fish fillets	500 g
2 tbsp	lemon juice	25 mL
	PARSLEY CHIVE SAUCE	
1 tbsp	butter	15 mL
1 tbsp	all-purpose flour	15 mL
1 cup	milk	250 mL
3/4 tsp	grated lemon rind	4 mL
2 tbsp	chopped fresh parsley	25 mL
1 tbsp	chopped fresh chives or green onion tops	15 mL
1/4 tsp	pepper	1 mL
Pinch	salt	Pinch

● PARSLEY CHIVE SAUCE: In 4-cup (1 L) microwaveable measure, microwave butter at High for 30 seconds or until melted. Stir in flour; microwave at High for 1 minute, stirring once. Whisk in milk and lemon rind; microwave at High for 5 to 7 minutes or until boiling and thickened, whisking frequently. Let stand for 1 minute. Stir in parsley, chives, pepper and salt.

● Meanwhile, in shallow dish, combine bread crumbs, salt and pepper. Brush fillets all over with lemon juice; dip into crumb mixture, turning to coat all over. Place on greased baking sheet; broil for about 5 minutes or until fish is opaque, golden and flakes easily when tested with fork. Serve with sauce. Makes 4 servings.

Microwaving the sauce while the fish broils frees your hands to toss the salad because you don't have to stir the sauce continuously.

Per serving: about
- 255 calories
- 32 g protein
- 6 g fat
- 15 g carbohydrate

TIP: If using frozen fish, individually frozen pieces are more expensive but more convenient. Block-frozen fillets are cheaper but tend to be irregular in size. Fresh fillets — surprisingly inexpensive and by far the most flavorful — are more even in size for easier cooking.

Glazed Fish Fillets ◀

4	halibut, haddock or cod fillets (1 lb/500 g)	4
1/3 cup	light mayonnaise	75 mL
4 tsp	pesto	20 mL

● Place fillets on greased or foil-lined rimmed baking sheet. Stir mayonnaise with pesto; spread over fish. Broil for about 5 minutes or until glaze is golden and bubbly and fish flakes easily when tested with fork. Makes 4 servings.

GLAZE VARIATIONS

Vary the flavor of Glazed Fish Fillets by substituting any of the following toppings. To 1/3 cup (75 mL) light mayonnaise, add:

● 2 tbsp (25 mL) finely chopped black olives, 1 tsp (5 mL) grated lemon rind, 1 tbsp (15 mL) lemon juice, 2 tsp (10 mL) chopped fresh thyme and pinch pepper.

● 4 tsp (20 mL) finely chopped oil-packed sun-dried tomatoes and 2 tsp (10 mL) chopped fresh parsley.

Mayonnaise blends with any number of flavors to give an instantly elegant glaze to fillets.

Per serving: about
- 193 calories
- 9 g fat
- 24 g protein
- 2 g carbohydrate

Tomato-Topped Haddock

4	haddock fillets (1 lb/500 g)	4
2 tbsp	olive oil	25 mL
2 tbsp	wine vinegar	25 mL
2	cloves garlic, minced	2
1/4 tsp	each salt and pepper	1 mL
2	plum tomatoes, thinly sliced	2
4 tsp	grated Parmesan cheese	20 mL
2 tsp	finely chopped fresh parsley	10 mL

● Arrange fillets side by side on greased or foil-lined rimmed baking sheet. Whisk together oil, vinegar, garlic, salt and pepper; brush half over fish. Lay tomato slices in row lengthwise over fish; brush with remaining oil mixture. Sprinkle with Parmesan cheese.

● Broil for about 5 minutes or until cheese is just golden and fish flakes easily when tested with fork. Serve sprinkled with parsley. Makes 4 servings.

Any other white fish fillets will also work well in this recipe. Served with buttered and parsley-speckled fettuccine.

Per serving: about
- 178 calories
- 8 g fat
- 23 g protein
- 2 g carbohydrate

Barbecued Red Snapper

4	red snapper fillets (4 oz/125 g each)	4
2 tbsp	chopped fresh parsley	25 mL
	SAUCE	
1	large sweet red pepper	1
1/4 cup	water or fish stock	50 mL
1 tsp	grated gingerroot	5 mL
1/2 tsp	pepper	2 mL
1/4 tsp	salt	1 mL
1/4 tsp	white wine vinegar	1 mL
Pinch	hot pepper flakes	Pinch

● SAUCE: Place red pepper on greased grill over medium-high heat or under broiler; close lid and cook, turning often, for about 15 minutes or until charred and puffed. Place in bowl; cover and let stand for 10 minutes. Peel and seed; purée in blender or food processor. Stir in water, ginger, pepper, salt, vinegar and hot pepper flakes. Set aside.

● Place fillets on greased grill over medium heat; close lid and cook, turning once, for about 8 minutes or until fish flakes easily when tested with fork. Sprinkle with parsley and serve with sauce. Makes 4 servings.

Round out the menu with green beans and new potatoes.

Per serving: about
- 115 calories
- 1 g fat
- 23 g protein
- 2 g carbohydrate

Swordfish with Country Vegetable Salad ▶

A *flavorful dressing does double duty in this easy, colorful meal. Use some of it for the vegetables and some as a marinade for the fish.*

Per serving: about
- 389 calories
- 23 g fat
- good source of iron
- 35 g protein
- 10 g carbohydrate

4	swordfish steaks (1-1/2 lb/750 g)	4
1	each sweet green and yellow pepper	1
1/3 cup	olive oil	75 mL
1/3 cup	red wine vinegar	75 mL
2 tbsp	chopped fresh oregano	25 mL
3	cloves garlic, minced	3
1/2 tsp	pepper	2 mL
2	tomatoes	2
1	piece (2 inches/5 cm) English cucumber	1
1/4 tsp	salt	1 mL
4	lemon wedges	4
4	leaves romaine lettuce	4

● Arrange fish in single layer in shallow glass dish. Core, seed and cut green and yellow peppers into 3/4-inch (2 cm) squares; place in bowl.

● Whisk together oil, vinegar, oregano, garlic and pepper; pour half over fish, turning to coat. Pour remaining oil mixture over sweet peppers. Cover each and marinate in refrigerator for at least 30 minutes or for up to 2 hours.

● Core and cut tomatoes into 1/2-inch (1 cm) cubes; add to peppers. Halve cucumber lengthwise; thinly slice crosswise and add to bowl along with half of the salt. Stir gently to coat.

● Discarding marinade, place fish on greased grill over medium-high heat; sprinkle with remaining salt. Close lid and cook, turning halfway through, for about 6 minutes or until fish is opaque and flakes easily when tested with fork. Squeeze juice from each lemon wedge over each steak.

● Place lettuce leaf on each plate; top with salad. Serve fish alongside. Makes 4 servings.

Pickerel Waves

S*weet and moist, freshwater pickerel strips are threaded onto skewers and served on a bed of spring greens tossed with vinaigrette.*

Per serving: about
- 200 calories
- 10 g fat
- 22 g protein
- 4 g carbohydrate

1 lb	pickerel fillets	500 g
1 tbsp	vegetable oil	15 mL
Pinch	each salt and pepper	Pinch
	CHIVE AND LEMON MAYO	
1/4 cup	light mayonnaise	50 mL
1/4 cup	light sour cream	50 mL
1 tbsp	minced fresh chives or green onion tops	15 mL
1/2 tsp	grated lemon rind	2 mL
2 tsp	lemon juice	10 mL
1/2 tsp	Dijon mustard	2 mL
Dash	hot pepper sauce	Dash
	Salt and pepper	

● CHIVE AND LEMON MAYO: In bowl, stir together mayonnaise, sour cream, chives, lemon rind and juice, mustard and hot pepper sauce; season with salt and pepper to taste. *(Mayo can be covered and refrigerated for up to 2 days.)*

● Cut pickerel into 3/4-inch (2 cm) wide strips; thread each strip onto soaked wooden skewer. Brush with oil; sprinkle with salt and pepper.

● Place skewers on greased grill over high heat; close lid and cook, turning once, for 2 to 6 minutes or until fish is golden, opaque and flakes easily when tested with fork. Pass Chive and Lemon Mayo separately. Makes 4 servings.

Cajun Fish Kabobs

A mix of spicy and hot makes Cajun one cool flavor. Fish prepared this quick way (photo, front cover) is low in fat and can be broiled when it's too cold outside to barbecue.

Per serving: about
- 185 calories
- 10 g fat
- 21 g protein
- 1 g carbohydrate

1 tbsp	olive oil	15 mL
1	clove garlic, minced	1
1 tsp	paprika	5 mL
3/4 tsp	pepper	4 mL
1/2 tsp	each dry mustard and dried oregano	2 mL
1/2 tsp	chili powder	2 mL
1/4 tsp	salt	1 mL
Pinch	cayenne pepper	Pinch
1 lb	salmon fillet, skinned	500 g

● In bowl, stir together oil, garlic, paprika, pepper, mustard, oregano, chili powder, salt and cayenne pepper.

● Cut salmon in 1-1/2-inch (4 cm) chunks; add to bowl and gently toss to coat evenly. Thread onto 4 soaked wooden skewers.

● Place kabobs on greased grill over medium heat; close lid and cook, turning once, for about 6 minutes or until opaque and fish flakes easily when tested with fork. Makes 4 servings.

Lemon Dill Halibut Kabobs

Firm-fleshed fish such as halibut, monkfish or salmon is best for kabobs because it is easy to skewer and won't fall apart while cooking.

Per serving: about
- 219 calories
- 7 g fat
- 36 g protein
- 2 g carbohydrate

1-1/2 lb	halibut or monkfish fillets	750 g
2 tsp	grated lemon rind	10 mL
1/4 cup	lemon juice	50 mL
2 tbsp	chopped fresh dill	25 mL
1 tbsp	vegetable oil	15 mL
2	cloves garlic, minced	2
1/4 tsp	each salt and pepper	1 mL

● Cut fillets into 1-inch (2.5 cm) chunks; place in bowl. Whisk together lemon rind and juice, dill, oil, garlic, salt and pepper; pour over fish and toss gently to coat. Thread onto eight 8-inch (20 cm) metal skewers.

● Place on greased grill over medium-high heat or under broiler; close lid and cook, turning once, for about 5 minutes or until fish is opaque and flakes easily when tested with fork. Makes 4 servings.

Barbecued Trout with Light Tartar Sauce

A handy grill basket that keeps fish intact while turning is especially useful for a delicate fish like trout. Otherwise, use two wide spatulas.

Per serving: about
- 285 calories
- 11 g fat
- 41 g protein
- 3 g carbohydrate

4	sprigs fresh dill	4
4	rainbow trout, cleaned (9 oz/260 g each)	4
	Salt and pepper	
	LIGHT TARTAR SAUCE	
1/4 cup	low-fat plain yogurt	50 mL
1/4 cup	light mayonnaise	50 mL
1/4 cup	finely chopped dill pickle	50 mL
2 tbsp	chopped fresh dill	25 mL
	Salt and pepper	

● Place dill sprig in each trout cavity; sprinkle cavity with salt and pepper to taste. Place on greased grill over high heat; close lid and cook, turning once, for 10 to 15 minutes or until fish flakes easily when tested with fork.

● LIGHT TARTAR SAUCE: Meanwhile, in bowl, stir together yogurt, mayonnaise, pickle, dill, and salt and pepper to taste; serve with fish. Makes 4 servings.

Tuna with Papaya Salad

6	tuna or salmon fillets, 3/4 inch (2 cm) thick (6 oz/175 g each)	6
1/4 cup	finely chopped shallots or onions	50 mL
1/4 cup	olive oil	50 mL
2 tbsp	lime juice or rice vinegar	25 mL
1 tbsp	minced gingerroot	15 mL
2 tsp	liquid honey	10 mL
1/4 tsp	sesame oil	1 mL
Pinch	salt	Pinch
	PAPAYA SALAD	
1	papaya	1
1	sweet red pepper	1
6 cups	torn mixed salad greens	1.5 L
1/2 cup	toasted chopped macadamia nuts or almonds	125 mL
1/4 cup	chopped green onions	50 mL

● Arrange fish in single layer in large shallow dish. Whisk together shallots, olive oil, lime juice, ginger, honey, sesame oil and salt. Spoon 1/4 cup (50 mL) over fish; turn to coat. Cover and marinate in refrigerator for 30 minutes.

● Place fish on greased grill over medium-high heat or under broiler on pan; close lid and grill for 4 to 5 minutes per side, or broil for 2 to 3 minutes per side, or just until opaque and fish flakes easily when tested with fork.

● PAPAYA SALAD: Meanwhile, peel papaya; seed and cut into 1/2-inch (1 cm) cubes. Seed and cut red pepper into 1/2-inch (1 cm) squares. In salad bowl, toss together papaya, red pepper, salad greens, nuts and green onions. Pour remaining lime juice mixture over top; toss to coat well. Arrange on serving plates; top with fish. Makes 6 servings.

B*ring the tropical taste of Hawaii to your table with this summer-fresh sensation.*

Per serving: about
- 455 calories
- 26 g fat
- good source of iron
- 42 g protein
- 13 g carbohydrate

TIP: If you can't find papaya, use 1-1/2 cups (375 mL) drained chopped canned peaches.

Halibut Steaks with Tomato Basil Sauce

2 tbsp	lemon juice	25 mL
1 tbsp	olive oil	15 mL
1 tsp	crushed dried rosemary	5 mL
	Salt and pepper	
4	halibut steaks	4
	TOMATO BASIL SAUCE	
1/2 cup	diced vine-ripe tomato	125 mL
1/4 cup	chopped fresh basil	50 mL
2 tbsp	finely chopped green onion	25 mL
1 tbsp	red wine vinegar	15 mL
1 tbsp	olive oil	15 mL
1/2 tsp	grated orange rind	2 mL
	Salt and pepper	

● Whisk together lemon juice, oil, rosemary, and salt and pepper to taste; pour into shallow glass dish. Add fish, turning to coat. Cover and let stand for 30 minutes or refrigerate for up to 4 hours.

● TOMATO BASIL SAUCE: Meanwhile, in bowl, stir together tomato, basil, onion, vinegar, oil, orange rind, and salt and pepper to taste.

● Place fish on greased grill over medium heat; close lid and cook, turning once, for about 10 minutes per inch (2.5 cm) of thickness or until fish is opaque and flakes easily when tested with fork. Spoon sauce over fish. Makes 4 servings.

F*resh tomatoes and herbs are an instant sauce for grilled or microwaved fish.*

Per serving: about
- 210 calories
- 6 g fat
- 36 g protein
- 1 g carbohydrate

Casseroles and Pies

When the occasion calls for something substantial, enjoy fish and seafood in hearty casseroles, tossed with spuds or blanketed in flaky pastry.

Salmon and Rice Pie ▶

With chunks of pink salmon, saffron-tinged rice and bright green asparagus, this pleasing pie is a dish fit for company.

Per each of 8 servings: about
- 470 calories
- 26 g fat
- good source of iron
- 22 g protein
- 35 g carbohydrate

1 cup	dry white wine	250 mL
1-3/4 cups	(approx) chicken or fish stock	425 mL
1-1/2 lb	boneless salmon	750 g
1/2 cup	parboiled rice	125 mL
Pinch	saffron (optional)	Pinch
8 oz	asparagus, trimmed (fresh or frozen)	250 g
	Pastry for deep 9-inch (23 cm) double-crust pie	
1	egg yolk	1
	SAUCE	
2 tbsp	butter	25 mL
1 cup	sliced mushrooms	250 mL
1/2 cup	minced onion	125 mL
2 tbsp	all-purpose flour	25 mL
Pinch	each salt and pepper	Pinch
2 tbsp	chopped fresh dill (or 2 tsp/10 mL dried dillweed)	25 mL

● In large deep skillet, bring wine and 1/2 cup (125 mL) of the stock to boil. Add salmon; cover and poach over medium heat for about 10 minutes or until firm to the touch but still translucent in center. With slotted lifter, transfer salmon to plate; let cool.

● Scrape off skin and grey fat layer; break salmon into large chunks and set aside. Strain poaching liquid into liquid measure; add enough stock to make 1-1/2 cups (375 mL). Set aside.

● Meanwhile, in saucepan, bring remaining 1-1/4 cups (300 mL) stock to boil; stir in rice, and saffron (if using). Return to boil; cover, reduce heat to low and cook for 20 minutes or until liquid is absorbed. Fluff with fork; let cool.

● In separate saucepan, cook asparagus in boiling water for 1 minute or until bright green; cool under cold water. Drain and pat dry; cut into 1-inch (2.5 cm) lengths.

● SAUCE: In heavy saucepan, melt butter over medium heat; cook mushrooms and onion, stirring often, for 5 minutes or until softened and liquid is evaporated. Sprinkle with flour; cook, stirring, for 1 minute without browning. Whisk in reserved poaching liquid; bring to boil. Reduce heat and simmer, stirring, for 3 minutes or until thickened. Season with salt and pepper; let cool. Stir in dill.

● On lightly floured surface, roll out half of the pastry and fit into deep 9-inch (23 cm) pie plate. Spoon rice over bottom. Top with salmon and asparagus; drizzle with sauce.

● Roll out remaining pastry to fit top. Beat egg yolk with 1 tsp (5 mL) water; brush some over pastry rim. Arrange pastry over top; trim and crimp edge. Brush with egg wash; cut attractive steam vents in top.

● Bake in bottom third of 425°F (220°C) oven for 15 minutes. Reduce heat to 375°F (190°C); bake for about 30 minutes or until golden brown and filling is steaming. Let stand on rack for 10 minutes before cutting. Makes 6 to 8 servings.

Lobster Quiche

Brenda Creighton of Prince Edward Island pleases her family every Christmas with this delicious no-fail quiche. An all-occasion dish, it's perfect for a casual potluck yet impressive enough for brunch or dinner guests.

Per serving: about
- 368 calories
- 13 g protein
- 27 g fat
- 20 g carbohydrate
- good source of calcium

1-1/2 cups	all-purpose flour	375 mL
1/2 tsp	salt	2 mL
1/4 cup	each cold butter and shortening, cubed	50 mL
1	egg yolk	1
1 tsp	white vinegar	5 mL
	FILLING	
1	can (4 oz/115 g) lobster meat	1
3/4 cup	whipping cream	175 mL
3	eggs	3
1 cup	shredded Jarlsberg cheese	250 mL

● In large bowl, combine flour with salt. Using pastry blender or two knives, cut in butter and shortening until mixture resembles coarse crumbs with a few larger pieces.

● In measuring cup, stir egg yolk with vinegar; add enough ice water to make 1/3 cup (75 mL). Sprinkle over flour mixture, stirring with fork until pastry holds together.

● Press pastry into disc; wrap in plastic wrap and refrigerate for at least 30 minutes or until chilled.

● On lightly floured surface, roll out pastry to 1/4-inch (5 mm) thickness; fit into 9-inch (23 cm) pie plate. Trim and flute edge. Line shell with foil or parchment paper; fill evenly with pie weights or dried beans.

● Bake in center of 375°F (190°C) oven for 15 minutes. Remove weights and foil; prick bottom and side all over with fork. Bake for 10 minutes or until bottom is light golden.

● FILLING: Meanwhile, drain lobster, reserving liquid in bowl; chop lobster meat coarsely. Add whipping cream and eggs to liquid; whisk until well combined. Stir in lobster.

● Sprinkle cheese over pie shell; pour in lobster mixture. Bake in center of 325°F (160°C) oven for about 45 minutes or until edge is set and center still slightly jiggly. Let stand for 5 minutes. Makes 8 servings.

TIP: Cans of lobster are also called hot pack. Check at gourmet stores or fish shops. If hot-pack lobster is not available, use entire can (11.3 oz/320 g) frozen lobster, draining and discarding liquid. Use 1 cup (250 mL) 18% cream instead of whipping cream and lobster juices.

Devilish Salmon Loaf

Every generation of cooks likes to whip up this classic using handy cans of salmon, and kids never say no to its comfy texture and taste.

Per serving: about
- 145 calories
- 16 g protein
- 6 g fat
- 6 g carbohydrate
- good source of calcium

2	cans (each 7-1/2 oz/213 g) salmon, drained	2
2	eggs, beaten	2
3/4 cup	milk	175 mL
1/3 cup	fine cracker crumbs	75 mL
1/3 cup	finely chopped celery	75 mL
1/4 cup	minced fresh parsley	50 mL
1/4 cup	finely chopped green onions	50 mL
3 tbsp	lemon juice	50 mL
1 tsp	dry mustard	5 mL
1/2 tsp	dried dillweed	2 mL
1/4 tsp	pepper	1 mL

● In large bowl, flake salmon and crush bones; add eggs and mix well. Stir in milk, crumbs, celery, parsley, onions, lemon juice, mustard, dill and pepper.

● Scrape into greased 8- x 4-inch (1.5 L) loaf pan; bake in 350°F (180°C) oven for about 1 hour or until knife inserted in center comes out clean. Makes 6 servings.

Smoked Salmon and Chèvre Quiche

1-2/3 cups	all-purpose flour	400 mL
Pinch	salt	Pinch
1/3 cup	cold butter, cubed	75 mL
1	egg yolk	1
1 tbsp	vegetable oil	15 mL
1/4 cup	(approx) cold water	50 mL
	FILLING	
1 tsp	vegetable oil	5 mL
4	green onions, sliced	4
3/4 tsp	dry mustard	4 mL
1/2 tsp	dried dillweed	2 mL
Pinch	pepper	Pinch
1 cup	milk	250 mL
1/2 cup	18% cream	125 mL
3	eggs	3
6 oz	smoked salmon, cut in small thin strips	175 g
1/3 cup	soft goat cheese, (chèvre), crumbled	75 mL

● In food processor or bowl, combine flour with salt; pulse or cut in butter with pastry blender or two knives until mixture resembles coarse crumbs with a few larger pieces.

● Stir egg yolk with oil; pour over flour mixture along with cold water. Pulse or stir together until mixture almost holds together, adding up to 1 tbsp (15 mL) more water if necessary. Press into ball; flatten into disc. Wrap in plastic wrap; refrigerate for at least 30 minutes or until chilled. *(Pastry can be refrigerated for up to 2 days.)*

● On lightly floured surface, roll out pastry to 1/4-inch (5 mm) thickness; fit into 9-inch (23 cm) pie plate. Trim and flute edge. Line shell with foil or parchment paper; fill evenly with pie weights or dried beans.

● Bake in center of 375°F (190°C) oven for 15 minutes. Remove weights and foil. Prick bottom and side all over with fork. Bake for 10 minutes or until bottom is light golden.

● FILLING: Meanwhile, in small nonstick skillet, heat oil over medium heat; cook onions, mustard, dillweed and pepper, stirring occasionally, for 3 minutes. Let cool for 5 minutes. In bowl, lightly whisk together milk, cream, eggs, onion mixture and smoked salmon; pour into prepared shell. Sprinkle with cheese.

● Bake in center of 350°F (180°C) oven for about 40 minutes or until edge is puffed and just starting to turn light golden and knife inserted in center comes out clean. Let stand for 10 minutes before serving. Makes 8 servings.

Follow this fail-proof pastry technique whenever making a single crust for a quiche.

Per serving: about
- 323 calories
- 20 g fat
- 13 g protein
- 23 g carbohydrate

TIP: Before making the filling for the quiche, taste the salmon. If it is salty, follow the recipe; if not, add a pinch of salt along with the pepper.

Clam Lasagna Roll-Ups

While lasagna does take time to prepare, the payoff is spending time with guests instead of attending to last-minute details in the kitchen.

Per serving (with Cream Sauce): about
- 468 calories
- 28 g protein
- 26 g fat
- 30 g carbohydrate
- excellent source of calcium and iron

6	lasagna noodles	6
	Cream Sauce (see box below)	
2 cups	shredded mozzarella cheese	500 mL
1/4 cup	freshly grated Parmesan cheese	50 mL
2 tbsp	fresh bread crumbs	25 mL
	CLAM SAUCE	
1 tbsp	olive oil	15 mL
1 cup	chopped onions	250 mL
2	cloves garlic, minced	2
1	can (28 oz/796 mL) tomatoes	1
2 tbsp	tomato paste	25 mL
2	cans (each 5 oz/142 g) baby clams	2
1 tsp	dried oregano	5 mL
1/4 tsp	hot pepper flakes	1 mL
2 tbsp	minced fresh parsley	25 mL
	Salt and pepper	
	FILLING	
2 cups	packed fresh spinach	500 mL
2	eggs	2
8 oz	ricotta cheese	250 g
1 cup	shredded mozzarella cheese	250 mL
1/2 cup	freshly grated Parmesan cheese	125 mL
2 tbsp	each chopped green onions and fresh parsley	25 mL
2 tbsp	chopped fresh basil (or 1 tsp/5 mL dried)	25 mL

● CLAM SAUCE: In heavy saucepan, heat oil over medium heat; cook onions and garlic, stirring occasionally, for 5 minutes or until softened. Add tomatoes, crushing with fork; add tomato paste.

● Drain clams, reserving 3/4 cup (175 mL) juice; set clams aside. Add juice to saucepan along with oregano and hot pepper flakes; bring to boil. Reduce heat and simmer for 25 minutes or until thick enough that space remains after drawing spoon across bottom of pan; let cool. Add clams, parsley, and salt and pepper to taste.

● FILLING: Rinse spinach, shaking off excess water. In saucepan, cook spinach over medium-high heat, with just the water clinging to leaves, for 4 minutes or until wilted. Press out moisture; chop finely and place in bowl. Mix in eggs, ricotta, mozzarella and Parmesan cheeses, onions, parsley and basil.

● In large pot of boiling salted water, cook noodles for 8 minutes or until tender. Drain and rinse in cold water. Drain and pat dry; cut in half.

● Spread about 3/4 cup (175 mL) of the clam sauce in 13- x 9-inch (3.5 L) baking dish. Working with half a noodle at a time, spread with about 3 tbsp (50 mL) filling, leaving 1 inch (2.5 cm) uncovered at one end. Spread about 2 tbsp (25 mL) clam sauce over filling. Starting at covered end, roll up and place, seam side down, in two rows on clam sauce in dish. Spread any remaining clam sauce around rolls.

● Pour Cream Sauce over rolls; sprinkle with mozzarella and Parmesan cheeses and bread crumbs. *(Lasagna can be prepared to this point, covered and refrigerated for up to 4 hours.)* Bake in 350°F (180°C) oven for 45 minutes or until bubbly and golden. Let stand for 10 minutes. Makes 8 servings.

CREAM SAUCE
● In small saucepan, melt 3 tbsp (50 mL) butter over medium heat. Blend in 3 tbsp (50 mL) all-purpose flour, 1/2 tsp (2 mL) salt, and pepper to taste; cook, whisking, for 1 minute. Gradually whisk in 1-1/2 cups (375 mL) milk; cook, whisking constantly, for 3 minutes or until boiling and thickened. Makes 1-3/4 cups (425 mL).

Herbed Seafood Casserole ▼

1 cup	long-grain rice	250 mL
1	egg, beaten	1
1/3 cup	chopped fresh parsley	75 mL
1/3 cup	butter	75 mL
1	onion, chopped	1
3	cloves garlic, minced	3
1	large carrot, finely chopped	1
1-1/2 cups	chopped fennel or celery	375 mL
1 tbsp	chopped fresh dill (or 1-1/2 tsp/7 mL dried dillweed)	15 mL
1 tsp	each salt and pepper	5 mL
1 lb	scallops	500 g
1 lb	raw shrimp, peeled and deveined	500 g
1	pkg (7 oz/200 g) frozen crabmeat, thawed	1
1/4 cup	all-purpose flour	50 mL
1-1/2 cups	milk	375 mL
1	pkg (8 oz/250 g) cream cheese	1
1/4 tsp	dried thyme	1 mL
	TOPPING	
1-1/2 cups	fresh bread crumbs	375 mL
2 tbsp	butter, melted	25 mL
	Sprigs fresh dill	

● In saucepan, combine rice with 2 cups (500 mL) salted water; bring to boil. Reduce heat to low; cover and simmer for 15 to 20 minutes or until tender and water is absorbed. Stir in egg and 2 tbsp (25 mL) of the parsley. Set aside.

● Meanwhile, in large skillet, melt 1 tbsp (15 mL) of the butter over medium heat; cook onion, garlic, carrot and fennel, stirring occasionally, for 3 to 5 minutes or until softened.

Stir in 1/2 tsp (2 mL) of the dill and 1/4 tsp (1 mL) each of the salt and pepper; transfer to large bowl.

● Wipe skillet clean. Pour in 2 cups (500 mL) water and bring to gentle simmer; poach scallops until just opaque, 1 to 3 minutes. Using slotted spoon, add scallops to bowl.

● Poach shrimp for about 3 minutes or until just pink. Drain, reserving 1 cup (250 mL) liquid. Add shrimp to bowl. Chop crabmeat into bite-size chunks; add to bowl.

● In same skillet, melt remaining butter over medium heat; whisk in flour and cook, whisking, for 2 minutes without browning. Gradually whisk in reserved poaching liquid and milk; cook, stirring, for about 5 minutes or until thickened. Whisk in cream cheese, thyme and remaining dill, salt and pepper until cheese is melted. Stir into seafood mixture along with remaining parsley.

● Line bottom of greased 13- x 9-inch (3.5 L) baking dish with rice mixture; spoon seafood mixture over top. (Casserole can be prepared to this point, covered and refrigerated for up to 2 days or frozen for up to 2 weeks; thaw in refrigerator for 48 hours.)

● TOPPING: Mix bread crumbs with butter; sprinkle over casserole. Bake in 325°F (160°C) oven for 40 to 50 minutes or until heated through and topping is golden and crunchy. Garnish with dill. Makes 8 servings.

A *rice crust holds a delectable blend of scallops, shrimp and crab in a herbed cream sauce. Definitely special, for a special occasion.*

Per serving: about
- 498 calories
- 25 g fat
- good source of iron
- 32 g protein
- 35 g carbohydrate

Tuna Fisherman's Pie

With cans of tuna on standby in the pantry, you can always whip up this comfy maritime version of shepherd's pie.

Per serving: about
- 310 calories
- 6 g fat
- good source of iron
- 29 g protein
- 36 g carbohydrate
- very high source of fiber

1 tbsp	vegetable oil	15 mL
1/2 cup	chopped celery	125 mL
6	green onions, sliced	6
3 tbsp	all-purpose flour	50 mL
2 cups	vegetable or chicken stock	500 mL
1/4 tsp	cayenne pepper	1 mL
	White pepper	
1 cup	frozen peas	250 mL
1	can (12 oz/341 mL) corn kernels	1
1/4 cup	chopped fresh parsley	50 mL
2	cans (each 7 oz/198 g) tuna, drained	2
1	egg white	1
3 cups	mashed cooked potatoes	750 mL
1/2 cup	freshly grated Parmesan cheese	125 mL
1 tbsp	fine dry bread crumbs	15 mL

● In nonstick saucepan, heat oil over medium heat; cook celery and onions, stirring, for 1 minute. Add 1 tbsp (15 mL) water; reduce heat to medium-low. Cover and cook for 4 minutes.

● Sprinkle with flour; cook, stirring, for 1 minute. Gradually stir in stock, cayenne and 1/4 tsp (1 mL) white pepper; cook over medium heat, stirring, until thickened. Stir in peas, undrained corn and parsley; remove from heat.

● Break tuna into chunks; add to vegetable mixture. Spoon into 10-cup (2.5 L) casserole or 9-inch (2.5 L) square baking dish.

● In bowl, lightly beat egg white; gradually mix in potatoes until smooth. Stir in Parmesan cheese and pinch of white pepper. Spoon over tuna mixture, spreading evenly; sprinkle with bread crumbs. Bake in 375°F (190°C) oven for 30 to 35 minutes or until golden brown and bubbly. Makes 6 servings.

Potato Tuna Melt for Two

Tuna melts deliciously on top of baking potatoes for suppers, weekend lunches or snacks. Use the microwave for speed, and double the recipe for unexpected company.

Per serving: about
- 370 calories
- 10 g fat
- good source of iron
- 27 g protein
- 43 g carbohydrate

2	large baking potatoes	2
1	can (6 oz/170 g) water-packed tuna	1
1/4 cup	light creamy cucumber salad dressing	50 mL
1	green onion, chopped	1
1	stalk celery, finely chopped	1
Pinch	each salt and pepper	Pinch
1/4 cup	shredded marble cheese	50 mL

● Scrub potatoes; pierce all over with fork. Microwave at High for about 6 minutes or until tender, rotating and turning potatoes halfway through. (Or bake in 400°F/200°C oven for 45 minutes.) Let stand for 5 minutes.

● Cut off one-quarter of each potato lengthwise. Scoop flesh from tops and 1-inch (2.5 cm) layer from each bottom. Place in bowl and mash with fork. Drain tuna; add to bowl, breaking up with fork. Stir in salad dressing, onion, celery, salt and pepper until combined.

● Place potato shells, cut side up, on baking sheet; mound tuna mixture on top. Sprinkle evenly with cheese. Broil for about 3 minutes or until filling is hot and cheese is bubbly. Makes 2 servings.

TIP: If doubling the recipe, increase the microwaving time for potatoes by 4 minutes.

Baked Salmon-Stuffed Potatoes

4	baking potatoes	4
1	can (7-1/2 oz/213 g) salmon, drained	1
1/2 cup	plain yogurt or sour cream	125 mL
1/4 cup	diced Cheddar cheese	50 mL
1 tbsp	chopped green onion	15 mL
1 tbsp	chopped fresh parsley or dill	15 mL
1 tbsp	lemon juice	15 mL
1/2 tsp	hot pepper sauce	2 mL
	Salt, pepper and paprika	
1/3 cup	shredded Cheddar cheese	75 mL

● Scrub potatoes; pierce all over with fork. Bake in 400°F (200°C) oven for 45 to 55 minutes or until tender; let stand for 5 minutes.

● Cut 1/2-inch (1 cm) thick slice lengthwise from each potato. Scoop out flesh from top and bottom, leaving 1/4-inch (5 mm) thick bottom shell. Place in bowl and mash with fork. Mix in salmon, yogurt, diced cheese, onion, parsley, lemon juice and hot pepper sauce; season with salt, pepper and paprika to taste.

● Place potato shells, cut side up, on baking sheet; spoon salmon mixture into shells, mounding tops. Sprinkle with shredded cheese. Bake in 400°F (200°C) oven for 15 to 20 minutes or until filling is hot and tops are crisp. Makes 4 servings.

T*he neat thing about this recipe is that you can bake and stuff the potatoes a day in advance, then simply reheat for lunch or supper the next day.*

Per serving: about
- 375 calories
- 13 g fat
- good source of iron
- 21 g protein
- 44 g carbohydrate
- excellent source of calcium

Smoked Salmon Strata

16	thin slices Italian-style bread	16
2 tbsp	butter	25 mL
1 cup	sliced leeks	250 mL
1 cup	sliced mushrooms	250 mL
4 oz	thinly sliced smoked salmon	125 g
2 cups	shredded Swiss cheese (about 8 oz/250 g)	500 mL
6	eggs	6
4 cups	18% cream	1 L
1 tsp	Dijon mustard	5 mL
	Pepper	

● Cut bread into cubes to make about 11 cups (2.75 L); set aside.

● In skillet, melt butter over medium heat; cook leeks and mushrooms, stirring occasionally, for 3 to 4 minutes or until leeks are softened. Remove from heat. Cut salmon crosswise into 1/2-inch (1 cm) wide strips; stir into leek mixture.

● In two greased 8-inch (2 L) square baking dishes, arrange half of the bread cubes. Top with salmon mixture, then half of the cheese; sprinkle with remaining bread cubes.

● Beat together eggs, cream, mustard, and pepper to taste; pour over layers. Sprinkle with remaining cheese. *(Strata can be covered and refrigerated for up to 12 hours.)*

● Bake in 325°F (160°C) oven for 35 to 45 minutes or until tops are golden. Serve hot. Makes 8 servings.

B*runch occasions don't leave much time to prepare. A strata that can be made the day before and kept in the fridge, ready to pop into the oven, is an ideal menu item. Smoked salmon makes the dish special-occasion.*

Per serving: about
- 544 calories
- 37 g fat
- excellent source of calcium
- 23 g protein
- 30 g carbohydrate

TIP: For a lighter touch, use milk instead of light cream.

Chicken and Shrimp Jambalaya ▲

As a dish for entertaining, jambalaya is hard to beat. Its variety of smoky meats, seafood, vegetables and herbs is sure to please everyone in the crowd — and, best of all, it's make-ahead.

Per serving: about
- 480 calories
- 8 g fat
- high source of fiber
- 39 g protein
- 62 g carbohydrate
- excellent source of iron

1 tbsp	butter	15 mL
2 cups	each chopped onion and celery	500 mL
1	sweet green pepper, chopped	1
3 oz	smoked sausage or ham, diced	90 g
1-1/2 lb	boneless skinless chicken breasts, cubed	750 g
1	clove garlic, minced	1
2	bay leaves	2
2 tsp	dried oregano	10 mL
1 tsp	dried thyme	5 mL
1/2 tsp	each salt, cayenne and black pepper	2 mL
1	can (28 oz/796 mL) tomatoes	1
1	can (7-1/2 oz/213 mL) tomato sauce	1
4 cups	chicken stock	1 L
2-1/2 cups	parboiled rice	625 mL
1 lb	raw shrimp, peeled and deveined	500 g
1	sweet red pepper, chopped	1
1/2 cup	each chopped green onions and fresh parsley	125 mL

● In Dutch oven, heat butter over medium-high heat; cook onion and celery, stirring occasionally, for 3 minutes. Add green pepper, sausage, chicken, garlic, bay leaves, oregano, thyme, salt, cayenne and black pepper; cook, stirring, for 2 minutes. Add tomatoes, tomato sauce and chicken stock; bring to boil. Stir in rice and shrimp; boil for 1 minute.

● Cover and bake in 350°F (180°C) oven for 25 minutes or until rice is tender. Discard bay leaves. Stir in red pepper and green onions; sprinkle with parsley. *(Jambalaya can be cooled, covered and refrigerated for up to 1 day. To reheat, stir in 1 cup/250 mL hot water; bake, covered, in 350°F/180°C oven for 1 hour and 15 minutes.)* Makes 8 servings.

Hearty Tuna Casserole

3 cups	rotini pasta	750 mL
2	cans (each 6-1/2 oz/184 g) chunk-style tuna, drained and flaked	2
1/2 cup	chopped celery	125 mL
2	green onions, sliced	2
2/3 cup	light sour cream	150 mL
1/2 cup	light mayonnaise	125 mL
2 tsp	Dijon mustard	10 mL
1/2 tsp	each dried thyme and salt	2 mL
1/4 tsp	pepper	1 mL
1	small zucchini, thinly sliced	1
1	tomato, sliced	1
1 cup	shredded Monterey Jack cheese	250 mL

● In large pot of boiling salted water, cook pasta for about 8 minutes or until tender but firm; drain and rinse. Drain well; return to pot.

● Add tuna, celery and onions; stir in sour cream, mayonnaise, mustard, thyme, salt and pepper.

● Spoon half of the tuna mixture into greased 8-cup (2 L) casserole; layer zucchini over top. Top with remaining tuna mixture. Arrange tomato slices over top; sprinkle with Monterey Jack cheese. Bake in 350°F (180°C) oven for 30 minutes or until hot and bubbly. Makes 4 servings.

*O*ur thanks to Lise Lapointe of Coaticook, Quebec, who sent in this tasty new take on tuna casserole for Canadian Living's 20th anniversary celebrations.

Per serving: about
- 550 calories
- 27 g fat
- good source of iron
- 37 g protein
- 39 g carbohydrate
- excellent source of calcium

Shrimp Pasta Bake

1 tbsp	olive oil	15 mL
2	cloves garlic, minced	2
1	onion, chopped	1
1 tsp	each dried basil and oregano	5 mL
1/2 tsp	each dried thyme and salt	2 mL
1/4 tsp	pepper	1 mL
1	can (28 oz/796 mL) tomatoes, puréed	1
1 tbsp	tomato paste	15 mL
1 lb	medium raw shrimp, peeled and deveined	500 g
1/4 cup	chopped fresh parsley	50 mL
2-1/2 cups	fusilli pasta	625 mL
4 oz	light cream cheese, softened	125 g
2/3 cup	light sour cream	150 mL
2	green onions, chopped	2
1/2 cup	shredded mozzarella cheese	125 mL
1/4 cup	freshly grated Parmesan cheese	50 mL

● In large saucepan, heat oil over medium heat; cook garlic, onion, basil, oregano, thyme, salt and pepper, stirring often, for 5 minutes or until softened.

● Add tomatoes and tomato paste; bring to boil. Reduce heat and simmer for about 15 minutes or until thickened slightly. Add shrimp; cook for about 5 minutes or until pink. Stir in parsley.

● Meanwhile, in large pot of boiling salted water, cook pasta for about 8 minutes or until tender but firm; drain well and add to sauce. Spread half in greased 11- x 7-inch (2 L) baking dish.

● In small bowl, beat cream cheese with sour cream until smooth; stir in onions. Spread over pasta mixture; top with remaining pasta mixture. Sprinkle with mozzarella and Parmesan cheeses. Cover with greased foil.

● Bake in 350°F (180°C) oven for about 1 hour or until bubbly and heated through. Uncover and broil for 2 minutes or until cheese is bubbly and golden. Makes 4 servings.

*P*asta, basking in tomato sauce studded with pink shrimp, bakes up crisp and welcoming. This recipe is quicker to make than a traditional lasagna.

Per serving: about
- 570 calories
- 21 g fat
- high source of fiber
- 37 g protein
- 59 g carbohydrate
- excellent source of calcium and iron

Pasta, Stews and Soups

Whether it's a quick toss with pasta or a deliciously long simmer in a soup or stew, the clean and fresh flavor of seafood shines in each of these delicious bowlfuls.

Company Shrimp and Noodles ▶

Sweet and sour Asian flavors and quick-cooking ingredients make this recipe ideal for a Friday night dinner with friends.

Per serving: about
- 440 calories
- 30 g protein
- 8 g fat
- 60 g carbohydrate
- high source of fiber
- excellent source of iron

1	onion	1
4 cups	snow peas, trimmed	1 L
8 oz	vermicelli noodles	250 g
2 tsp	vegetable oil	10 mL
3	cloves garlic, minced	3
2 tsp	minced gingerroot	10 mL
1 lb	large raw shrimp, peeled and deveined	500 g
1/2 cup	chicken stock	125 mL
1/4 cup	hoisin sauce	50 mL
1 tbsp	soy sauce	15 mL
2 tsp	rice vinegar	10 mL
1 tsp	cornstarch	5 mL
Dash	hot pepper sauce	Dash
2 tbsp	chopped unsalted roasted peanuts	25 mL

● Cut onion in half lengthwise; slice lengthwise into thin strips. Cut snow peas in half diagonally. Set onion and snow peas aside.

● In large pot of boiling salted water, cook noodles for 7 minutes or until tender but firm; drain.

● Meanwhile, in nonstick wok or large skillet, heat oil over medium-high heat; stir-fry onion, garlic and ginger for 2 minutes. Add shrimp and snow peas; stir-fry for 1 minute.

● Whisk together chicken stock, hoisin sauce, soy sauce, vinegar, cornstarch and hot pepper sauce; stir into shrimp mixture.

● Increase heat to high; stir-fry for 3 minutes or until shrimp are firm and pink and sauce is thickened. Add noodles and toss to combine. Sprinkle with peanuts. Makes 4 servings.

TIP: Use wide noodles, if you like (as we did in the photograph).

Linguine with Clams and Tomatoes ◀

1 tsp	each vegetable oil and butter	5 mL
1	large onion, chopped	1
1	clove garlic, minced	1
1	can (10 oz/283 g) baby clams	1
1/2 cup	white wine, apple juice or white grape juice	125 mL
1	can (19 oz/540 mL) tomatoes	1
2 tsp	each dried oregano and basil	10 mL
1/2 tsp	each salt and pepper	2 mL
12 oz	linguine pasta	375 g
1/4 cup	freshly grated Parmesan cheese	50 mL

● In saucepan, heat oil and butter over medium heat; cook onion and garlic, stirring occasionally, for 5 minutes or until softened.

● Drain clams, reserving 1/4 cup (50 mL) liquid; set clams aside. Add liquid and wine to saucepan; cook, stirring occasionally, for 2 minutes or until reduced slightly. Add tomatoes, oregano, basil, salt and pepper, breaking up tomatoes into small pieces; cook for about 10 minutes or until thickened. Add clams; cook until steaming hot.

● Meanwhile, in saucepan of boiling salted water, cook pasta for 8 to 10 minutes or until tender but firm; drain well and return to pot. Add clam mixture and toss to coat. Serve sprinkled with Parmesan cheese. Makes 4 servings.

This very light, clean sauce features an abundance of clams. Canned do very nicely — but you can also up the taste by using fresh.

Per serving: about
- 475 calories
- 7 g fat
- high source of fiber
- excellent source of iron
- 25 g protein
- 76 g carbohydrate
- good source of calcium

TIP: To make linguine with fresh clams (as we did for our photo), omit clam liquid. Cook sauce for 15 minutes. Scrub 2 lb (1 kg) clams, discarding any that do not close; add instead of canned clams and cook, covered, for 7 to 10 minutes or until shells open. Discard any that do not open.

Linguine with Creamy Clam Sauce

2	cans (each 5 oz/142 g) baby clams	2
1	onion, finely chopped	1
2	cloves garlic, minced	2
1/4 tsp	dried thyme	1 mL
Pinch	hot pepper flakes (optional)	Pinch
2-1/2 cups	cubed zucchini	625 mL
1	large sweet red pepper, diced	1
4 oz	light cream cheese, cubed	125 g
1/2 tsp	salt	2 mL
1/4 tsp	pepper	1 mL
12 oz	linguine pasta	375 g
1/4 cup	freshly grated Parmesan cheese	50 mL
2 tbsp	chopped fresh parsley	25 mL

● Drain clams, reserving liquid; set clams aside. In large skillet, cook 1/3 cup (75 mL) of the clam liquid, onion, garlic, thyme, and hot pepper flakes (if using) over medium heat, stirring occasionally, for about 5 minutes or until onion is softened. Add zucchini and red pepper; cook for about 3 minutes or until zucchini is tender-crisp.

● Add remaining clam liquid; increase heat to medium-high. Stir in cream cheese; cook, stirring, for 3 minutes or until sauce is slightly thickened. Add clams, salt and pepper; stir until heated through.

● Meanwhile, in large pot of boiling salted water, cook linguine for 8 to 10 minutes or until tender but firm; drain well and return to pot. Add sauce and Parmesan; toss to coat. Serve sprinkled with parsley. Makes 4 servings.

Light cream cheese thickens a quick sauce to serve over linguine or other long pasta.

Per serving: about
- 505 calories
- 11 g fat
- good source of calcium
- very high source of fiber
- 25 g protein
- 75 g carbohydrate
- excellent source of iron

Linguine with Scallops and Spinach

This wonderfully easy dish delivers a good source of calcium and an excellent source of iron.

Per serving: about
- 460 calories
- 9 g fat
- good source of calcium
- 33 g protein
- 64 g carbohydrate
- excellent source of iron

8 oz	linguine pasta	250 g
1/2 cup	chicken stock or white wine	125 mL
1	onion, minced	1
8 oz	scallops	250 g
1/3 cup	light cream cheese	75 mL
2 tbsp	chopped fresh dill (or 1 tsp/5 mL dried basil)	25 mL
1 tsp	grated lemon rind	5 mL
2 cups	shredded fresh spinach	500 mL
	Salt and pepper	
2 tbsp	freshly grated Parmesan cheese	25 mL

● In large pot of boiling salted water, cook linguine for 8 to 10 minutes or until tender but firm; drain and return to pot.

● Meanwhile, in small saucepan, bring chicken stock to simmer. Add onion and scallops; cook for about 4 minutes or until scallops are opaque. Using slotted spoon, transfer scallops to bowl and keep warm.

● Add cream cheese, dill and lemon rind to cooking liquid; cook over medium heat, stirring, until smooth. Add to pasta and toss to coat. Add spinach and scallops; toss to combine. Season with salt and pepper to taste. Serve sprinkled with Parmesan cheese. Makes 3 servings.

Singapore Shrimp Noodles

From food writer Bonnie Stern comes this delicious way to enjoy shrimp without spending a fortune. You can serve the dish hot or at room temperature.

Per serving: about
- 400 calories
- 9 g fat
- good source of iron
- 17 g protein
- 63 g carbohydrate

8 oz	rice vermicelli noodles	250 g
8 oz	raw shrimp	250 g
1 tbsp	vegetable oil	15 mL
3	cloves garlic, finely chopped	3
1 tbsp	minced gingerroot	15 mL
3	green onions, finely chopped	3
1 tbsp	curry powder	15 mL
1	onion, thinly sliced	1
1	carrot, grated	1
1	sweet red pepper, thinly sliced	1
4 oz	bean sprouts	125 g
4 oz	snow peas, trimmed	125 g
	SAUCE	
1/2 cup	chicken stock or water	125 mL
2 tbsp	soy sauce	25 mL
1 tbsp	granulated sugar	15 mL
1 tbsp	each sesame oil and rice wine	15 mL
2 tsp	cornstarch	10 mL

● Soak noodles in hot water for 20 minutes or until softened; drain and set aside. Peel shrimp. Starting at top of outer curve, cut three-quarters of the way through shrimp and open to butterfly; discard vein. Set aside.

● SAUCE: Combine chicken stock, soy sauce, sugar, oil, rice wine and cornstarch; set aside.

● In wok or large deep skillet, heat oil over medium-high heat; stir-fry garlic, ginger and green onions for 30 seconds or until fragrant. Add curry powder; stir-fry for 10 seconds. Add onion, carrot and red pepper; cook, stirring occasionally, for 3 to 4 minutes or until slightly wilted. Stir in shrimp.

● Stir sauce and add to pan; bring to boil. Cook for about 1-1/2 minutes or just until shrimp turn pink. Add bean sprouts, snow peas and noodles; cook, tossing well, for about 2 minutes or until thoroughly heated. Makes 4 servings.

TIP: You can use angel hair pasta as an alternative to rice vermicelli. Cook ahead according to package directions, then rinse and toss with 1 tbsp (15 mL) sesame oil.

Mediterranean-Style Tuna ▲

1/2 cup	prepared Caesar salad dressing	125 mL
1	onion, chopped	1
3	cloves garlic, minced	3
1	can (6.5 oz/184 g) water-packed solid or chunk tuna, drained	1
1/2 cup	sliced black olives	125 mL
1 tbsp	crumbled dried basil	15 mL
1/4 tsp	hot pepper flakes	1 mL
1 cup	chopped tomato	250 mL
5 oz	feta cheese, cut in 1/2-inch (1 cm) cubes	150 g
8 oz	spaghetti	250 g

● In skillet, heat salad dressing over medium heat. Add onion and garlic; cook, stirring occasionally, for 5 minutes or until softened. Add tuna, breaking up into large chunks.

● Add olives, basil and hot pepper flakes; cook for 2 minutes. Add tomato and feta cheese; cook just until warmed through and cheese cubes melt just at edges, about 1 minute.

● Meanwhile, in saucepan of boiling salted water, cook spaghetti for 8 to 10 minutes or until tender but firm; drain well and return to pot. Add sauce and gently toss to coat. Makes 4 servings.

F*amily-friendly, fast and tasty — these are the criteria the Test Kitchen uses to judge entries in our annual Newman's Own Recipe Contest that raises considerable money for the Canadian Living Foundation for Families, Breakfast for Learning. Here's Ann Teeter's 1997 grand-prize recipe.*

Per serving: about
- 550 calories
- 27 g fat
- high source of fiber
- 25 g protein
- 51 g carbohydrate
- good source of calcium and iron

Corn and Smoked Salmon Chowder ◄

2	each sweet red and green peppers	2
1/4 cup	butter	50 mL
2	each carrots and onions, diced	2
2	leeks, sliced	2
1/2 cup	sliced celery	125 mL
4	cloves garlic, minced	4
4	potatoes, peeled and diced	4
1/4 cup	all-purpose flour	50 mL
2 tsp	dried thyme	10 mL
Pinch	each salt and pepper	Pinch
5 cups	clam juice, fish stock or chicken stock (or combination)	1.25 L
1	pkg (2 lb/1 kg) frozen corn kernels	1
2 cups	milk	500 mL
2 cups	10% cream	500 mL
4 oz	smoked salmon, julienned	125 g
	Chopped fresh dill	

● Broil red and green peppers, turning often, for 20 to 30 minutes or until charred all over. Let cool; peel, seed and dice. Set aside.

● In large Dutch oven, melt butter over medium-low heat; cook carrots, onions, leeks, celery and garlic, stirring occasionally, for about 15 minutes or until softened but not browned.

● Add potatoes, flour, thyme, salt and pepper; cook, stirring, for 1 minute. Add clam juice; bring to boil. Reduce heat, cover and simmer for about 10 minutes or just until potatoes are barely tender.

● Add corn and roasted peppers; cook over high heat, stirring, for 6 minutes. Reduce heat to low; simmer for 5 minutes. *(Chowder can be prepared to this point, cooled in refrigerator and stored in airtight container for up to 24 hours; reheat gently before continuing.)*

● Stir in milk and cream; heat through but do not boil. Ladle into heated bowls; garnish with salmon and dill. Makes 8 servings.

Roasted red peppers add a lively twist to a hearty chowder that's special enough for any entertaining occasion.

Per serving: about
- 379 calories
- 14 g fat
- high source of fiber
- 13 g protein
- 56 g carbohydrate
- good source of calcium and iron

Easy Salmon Chowder

2 tbsp	butter or vegetable oil	25 mL
1/2 cup	each chopped onions and celery	125 mL
1/4 cup	chopped sweet green pepper	50 mL
1	clove garlic, minced	1
3 cups	diced peeled potatoes	750 mL
2 cups	chicken stock	500 mL
1 cup	diced carrots	250 mL
3/4 tsp	pepper	4 mL
1/2 cup	diced zucchini	125 mL
1	can (7-1/2 oz/213 g) sockeye salmon	1
1 cup	corn kernels	250 mL
1 cup	evaporated milk	250 mL
2 tbsp	chopped fresh dill	25 mL
	Salt	

● In large heavy saucepan, melt butter over medium-low heat; cook onions, celery, green pepper and garlic, stirring occasionally, for about 5 minutes or until softened.

● Add potatoes, stock, carrots and pepper; bring to boil. Reduce heat, cover and simmer for 8 minutes or just until vegetables are tender. Add zucchini; cook for 5 minutes.

● Meanwhile, drain salmon, reserving juice; break into large chunks, crushing bones and removing skin, if desired. Add salmon, reserved juice, corn and milk to pan; heat through. Garnish with dill and season with salt to taste. Makes 4 servings.

Keep a can of salmon in the cupboard so you can make this excellent chowder, full of chunky vegetables, for a cold-weather lunch or supper.

Per serving: about
- 385 calories
- 13 g fat
- good source of iron
- excellent source of calcium
- 22 g protein
- 46 g carbohydrate
- high source of fiber

Mom's Best Qualicum Chowder ▶

Sondra Mawdsley, the West Coast winner of our 1998 Great Home-Cooking Mom Contest, not only cooks up a tremendous chowder but also catches the fish for it!

Per each of 6 servings: about
- 244 calories
- 8 g fat
- good source of iron
- 25 g protein
- 14 g carbohydrate

1 lb	mussels	500 g
1-1/2 cups	water	375 mL
1 cup	dry white wine	250 mL
2	cloves garlic	2
2 tbsp	butter	25 mL
1	large potato, peeled and diced	1
2	carrots, diced	2
2 tbsp	all-purpose flour	25 mL
1/2 tsp	each salt and pepper	2 mL
2	tomatoes, chopped	2
12 oz	salmon fillet	375 g
4 oz	each sole, cod and snapper fillets	125 g
2 tbsp	chopped fresh parsley	25 mL
2 tbsp	chopped fresh chives or green onions	25 mL

● Scrub mussels, removing any beards; discard any that do not close when tapped. In Dutch oven, bring 1/2 cup (125 mL) of the water, the wine and garlic to simmer over medium-high heat. Add mussels; cover and steam for about 5 minutes or until mussels open. Discard any that do not open.

● Strain mussels, reserving liquid and garlic; let cool. Mince garlic; set aside. Remove mussels from shells, reserving 4 to 6 intact; set aside.

● In Dutch oven, heat butter over medium heat; cook reserved garlic, potato and carrots, stirring occasionally, for about 8 minutes or until softened. Sprinkle with flour; cook, stirring, for 1 minute. Whisk in reserved liquid from mussels, remaining water, salt and pepper; bring to boil. Add tomatoes; reduce heat and simmer for 10 minutes.

● Cut salmon, sole, cod and snapper into 1-inch (2.5 cm) pieces; add to pan. Cover and cook for about 8 minutes or until fish flakes easily when tested with fork. Add mussels and mussels in shells; heat through. Ladle into warmed bowls. Garnish each with 1 mussel in shell, parsley and chives. Makes 4 to 6 servings.

Maritime Lobster Chowder

If using frozen lobster (one 11.3 oz/320 g can), an excellent product available year-round across the country, thaw in the refrigerator, drain and reserve juices.

Per serving: about
- 298 calories
- 18 g fat
- 15 g protein
- 19 g carbohydrate

6 cups	diced peeled potatoes (about 8)	1.5 L
2	large onions, diced	2
3 cups	lobster meat (about 4 lobsters, each 1-1/2 lb/750 g, cooked and juices reserved)	750 mL
1/4 cup	butter	50 mL
2 cups	18% cream	500 mL
1 cup	whipping cream	250 mL
1-1/2 cups	lobster juice, fish stock or canned clam juice	375 mL
	Salt and pepper	

● In large pot, bring 3 cups (750 mL) water to boil over medium-high heat; add potatoes and onions. Cover and cook for 5 to 10 minutes or just until potatoes are tender. Do not drain.

● Meanwhile, cut lobster into bite-size pieces. In large skillet, heat 2 tbsp (25 mL) of the butter over medium-high heat; cook lobster, stirring occasionally, for 3 to 5 minutes or until light golden.

● Add lobster to potato mixture along with 18% cream, whipping cream, lobster juice and remaining butter. Cook over medium heat for 3 to 5 minutes or just until heated through but not boiling. Season with salt and pepper to taste. Makes 12 servings.

Mussel Soup Italiano ▲

Warm up a winter's evening with a bowlful of zesty mussels by the fire.

Per serving: about
- 134 calories
- 7 g protein
- 8 g fat
- 8 g carbohydrate
- good source of iron

2 tbsp	each butter and vegetable oil	25 mL
1	onion, chopped	1
2	cloves garlic, minced	2
1 cup	dry white wine or chicken stock	250 mL
1	can (28 oz/796 mL) tomatoes	1
1 tbsp	lemon juice	15 mL
1-1/2 tsp	dried basil	7 mL
3 lb	mussels	1.5 kg

● In large heavy saucepan or Dutch oven, heat butter with oil over medium-high heat; cook onion and garlic, stirring occasionally, for about 5 minutes or until softened.

● Add wine, tomatoes, lemon juice and basil, crushing tomatoes with fork; bring to boil. Reduce heat and simmer for 5 minutes.

● Meanwhile, scrub mussels, removing any beards; discard any that do not close when tapped. Add to pan; cover and cook for 5 to 7 minutes or until mussels open. Discard any that do not open. Makes 8 servings.

Easy Cioppino

1 tbsp	olive oil	15 mL
1 cup	chopped onions	250 mL
1 cup	chopped sweet green pepper	250 mL
1/2 cup	chopped celery	125 mL
4	cloves garlic, minced	4
1	can (28 oz/796 mL) tomatoes	1
3 cups	tomato-clam cocktail juice	750 mL
1/2 cup	dry white wine or water	125 mL
2	bay leaves	2
1/2 tsp	each dried thyme and oregano	2 mL
Pinch	hot pepper flakes (optional)	Pinch
	Salt and pepper	
1-1/2 lb	clams	750 g
2 lb	mussels	1 kg
8 oz	large raw shrimp, peeled and deveined	250 g

● In large heavy saucepan, heat oil over medium heat; cook onions, green pepper, celery and garlic, stirring occasionally, for 5 minutes.

● Add tomatoes, breaking up with spoon. Stir in cocktail juice, wine, bay leaves, thyme, oregano, and hot pepper flakes (if using); bring to boil. Cover, reduce heat and simmer, stirring occasionally, for 30 minutes. Discard bay leaves. Season with salt and pepper to taste.

● Scrub clams and mussels under cold running water, removing any beards. Discard any that do not close when tapped. Add clams to pot; cook, covered, for 5 minutes. Add mussels; cook, covered, for 5 minutes or until shells open. Add shrimp; cook for 2 minutes or until pink. Discard any clams or mussels that do not open. Makes 6 servings.

As easy as everyday cooking but with an entertaining twist, this lusty tomato stew/soup always rates raves from guests.

Per serving: about
- 210 calories
- 5 g fat
- excellent source of iron
- 16 g protein
- 26 g carbohydrate

Tomato Mussel Chowder

2 tbsp	olive oil	25 mL
2	cloves garlic, minced	2
1	each onion, carrot and stalk celery, chopped	1
1	sweet green or yellow pepper, chopped	1
1	zucchini, diced	1
1	can (28 oz/796 mL) stewed tomatoes	1
1	bottle (237 mL) clam juice (or 1 cup/250 mL fish stock)	1
1 tsp	dried basil	5 mL
1/2 tsp	fennel seeds, crushed	2 mL
1/4 tsp	each dried thyme, cayenne and black pepper	1 mL
1-1/2 lb	mussels	750 g
1/3 cup	each chopped green onions and fresh parsley	75 mL

● In large saucepan, heat oil over medium heat; cook garlic, onion, carrot and celery, stirring occasionally, for 5 minutes. Add green pepper and zucchini; cook for 5 minutes.

● Add tomatoes, clam juice, basil, fennel seeds, thyme, cayenne and black pepper; bring to boil, stirring. Reduce heat and simmer for 20 minutes or until thickened.

● Meanwhile, scrub mussels, removing any beards. Discard any that do not close when tapped. Add to tomato mixture; cover and cook for 5 minutes or until mussels open. Discard any mussels that do not open. Ladle into warmed shallow bowls; sprinkle with green onions and parsley. Makes 4 servings.

Try this lusty bowlful of mussels with toasty focaccia or garlic bread.

Per serving: about
- 220 calories
- 9 g fat
- high source of fiber
- excellent source of iron
- 13 g protein
- 26 g carbohydrate
- good source of calcium

Clams in Coriander Sauce ▶

This easy entertaining recipe originated in Toronto's Portuguese community. Make sure you have lots of crusty bread for mopping up every last delicious bit.

Per each of 6 servings: about
- 105 calories
- 9 g fat
- good source of iron
- 3 g protein
- 1 g carbohydrate

2 lb	Manila clams	1 kg
2 tbsp	butter	25 mL
2 tbsp	olive oil	25 mL
3	cloves garlic, minced	3
2/3 cup	dry white wine	150 mL
3	bay leaves	3
Pinch	each salt and pepper	Pinch
1/3 cup	minced fresh coriander	75 mL
	Lemon wedges	

● Scrub clams under cold running water; discard any that do not close when tapped. In large heavy saucepan, heat butter with oil over medium-high heat; cook garlic for about 1 minute or until softened.

● Add clams, wine, bay leaves, salt and pepper; cover and cook for 5 to 7 minutes or until shells open. Discard any clams that do not open. Stir in coriander. Ladle into warmed bowls; serve with lemon to squeeze over top. Makes 4 to 6 servings.

Grouper in Coconut Curry Sauce

Take your taste buds on a fantasy trip to the Caribbean for a dish that combines the best of fresh fish, lively curry, tropical fruit and creamy coconut.

Per serving: about
- 327 calories
- 15 g fat
- excellent source of iron
- 35 g protein
- 14 g carbohydrate

2 tbsp	vegetable oil	25 mL
1	each onion and apple, finely chopped	1
2	cloves garlic, minced	2
1 tbsp	minced gingerroot	15 mL
1 tbsp	curry powder	15 mL
1/2 tsp	ground cumin	2 mL
1 cup	canned unsweetened coconut milk	250 mL
1/2 cup	chicken stock	125 mL
2 tbsp	tomato paste	25 mL
1/4 tsp	salt	1 mL
6	grouper, swordfish or halibut fillets, 3/4 inch (2 cm) thick (6 oz/175 g each)	6
	GARNISH	
1	mango (or 1 cup/250 mL diced canned peaches)	1
1/4 cup	chopped fresh coriander or parsley	50 mL

● In large skillet, heat oil over medium heat; cook onion, apple, garlic and ginger, stirring occasionally, for 5 minutes or until softened. Add curry powder and cumin; cook, stirring, for 30 seconds.

● Mix in coconut milk, stock, tomato paste and salt; cook for 5 minutes or until slightly thickened. Nestle fillets in mixture; cover and cook for 5 minutes.

● Turn fish over; cook, uncovered, for 5 minutes or until sauce is thickened and fish is opaque and flakes easily when tested with fork.

● GARNISH: Peel, pit and cube mango. Garnish each serving with mango and coriander. Makes 6 servings.

TIP: To cube a mango, cut off vertical slice from each narrow side; discard pit. Cut grid pattern in flesh of each side down to (but not through) skin. Gently push skin to turn inside out; cut off flesh. Cut flesh off vertical slices.

Shrimp and Rice Soup ◄

8 oz	fresh or frozen shrimp, peeled and deveined	250 g
1/3 cup	minced shallots or green onions	75 mL
4	cloves garlic, minced	4
2 tbsp	fish sauce	25 mL
1/2 tsp	pepper	2 mL
4 cups	chicken stock	1 L
1 cup	Thai jasmine rice or other long-grain white rice	250 mL
4	stalks lemongrass (or 4 tsp/20 mL grated lemon rind)	4
1 tbsp	vegetable oil	15 mL
2	tomatoes, chopped	2
	GARNISHES	
2 tbsp	coarsely chopped dry-roasted unsalted peanuts	25 mL
1 cup	fresh coriander leaves (optional)	250 mL
1	hot red or green chili pepper, minced (optional)	1
	Vietnamese Dipping Sauce (see box below)	

● Coarsely chop shrimp. In bowl, whisk together shallots, one-quarter of the garlic, the fish sauce and pepper. Add shrimp; toss to coat. Set aside.

● In large stockpot, combine stock, 4 cups (1 L) water and rice; bring to boil.

● Meanwhile, peel tough outer layers from lemongrass; using side of knife or meat pounder, smash stalks and add to rice along with another one-quarter of the garlic. Reduce heat to medium; simmer, partially covered, for 15 minutes.

● Meanwhile, in small skillet, heat oil over medium heat; stir-fry remaining garlic for 30 seconds or until golden. Add shrimp mixture; stir-fry for about 1 minute or until shrimp starts to turn pink. Add to rice mixture along with tomatoes; simmer for 5 minutes. Discard lemongrass. Ladle into bowls.

● GARNISHES: Serve with peanuts, coriander leaves (if using), chili pepper (if using) and Vietnamese Dipping Sauce. Makes 6 servings.

P*ass the garnishes in small bowls to accompany this aromatic Vietnamese soup.*

Per serving (without Dipping Sauce): about
- 225 calories
- 6 g fat
- 13 g protein
- 30 g carbohydrate

TIP: Thai jasmine rice is a long-grain white rice with a subtle nutty scent. It is available in specialty, Asian and health food stores and some supermarkets.

VIETNAMESE DIPPING SAUCE

● In bowl, whisk together 1/4 cup (50 mL) Vietnamese or Thai fish sauce, 1/4 cup (50 mL) water, 3 tbsp (50 mL) lime juice, 1 tbsp (15 mL) granulated sugar, 1 minced clove garlic and pinch hot pepper flakes. Makes 6 servings.

Per serving: about • 15 calories • 1 g protein • 0 g fat • 3 g carbohydrate

Light Bites

These days, we're doing more grazing, snacking and indulging in appetizers — and seafood suits this new way of eating to a T.

Swordfish and Olive Mayonnaise Sandwich ▶

This is one fabulous sandwich from food writer Bonnie Stern — thin slices of meaty swordfish and roasted red peppers seasoned with fresh basil, rosemary and an olive-studded mayonnaise.

Per serving: about
- 390 calories
- 23 g protein
- 18 g fat
- 35 g carbohydrate
- good source of iron

12 oz	swordfish	375 g
2 tbsp	olive oil	25 mL
1 tbsp	chopped fresh rosemary	15 mL
1	clove garlic, minced	1
1/2 tsp	salt	2 mL
1/4 tsp	pepper	1 mL
8	thin slices bread (or 4 buns)	8
2	roasted sweet red peppers, thinly sliced	2
12	large basil leaves	12
	OLIVE MAYONNAISE	
1/4 cup	pitted black olives	50 mL
1/4 cup	light mayonnaise or low-fat plain yogurt	50 mL
1/4 tsp	pepper	1 mL
1	clove garlic, minced	1

● Pat fish dry. With sharp knife, slice horizontally into 1/4-inch (5 mm) thick slices; place in shallow dish.

● Whisk together oil, rosemary, garlic, salt and pepper; brush over fish, turning to coat. Marinate for 10 minutes at room temperature or cover and refrigerate for up to 1 hour.

● OLIVE MAYONNAISE: Meanwhile, in blender, purée together olives, mayonnaise, pepper and garlic; set aside.

● Place fish on greased grill over medium-high heat or under broiler; close lid and cook for 2 minutes per side or until fish is opaque and flakes easily when tested with fork.

● Lightly toast bread. Evenly spread olive mayonnaise over 1 side of each slice. Arrange fish evenly over 4 of the slices; top with red peppers and basil. Sandwich with remaining bread, mayonnaise side down. Makes 4 servings.

COOKED TO PERFECTION

Whether fish is large or small, in steaks or fillets, the same cooking rule applies — 10 minutes for every 1 inch (2.5 cm) of thickness. Fish is perfectly cooked just when it passes from translucence to opaqueness and the flesh flakes easily when gently probed with a fork but is still moist. (Add about 10 minutes if fish is wrapped in foil or parchment paper packets.) Here are some temperature guidelines.

● Grill over medium-high heat, turning once. (Do not grill if fish is less than 3/4 inch/2 cm thick.)

● Steam or poach in gently simmering liquid in covered pan.

● Broil about 4 inches (10 cm) from heat, turning once if thicker than 3/4 inch (2 cm).

● Pan-fry over medium-high heat (medium, if breaded), turning once.

● Bake in 450°F (230°C) oven.

Smoked Salmon Rolls on Mixed Greens

Vancouver is a rich source of excellent fish dishes — including this tortilla salmon roll nestled on dressed greens, a specialty of Dufour & Co.

Per serving: about
- 345 calories
- 11 g protein
- 23 g fat
- 26 g carbohydrate
- good source of iron

1/4 cup	cream cheese, softened	50 mL
1 tbsp	chopped fresh chives	15 mL
1	clove garlic, chopped	1
1 tsp	minced gingerroot	5 mL
Pinch	each salt and pepper	Pinch
4	6-inch (15 cm) flour tortillas	4
12	thin slices smoked salmon (about 4 oz/125 g)	12
8 cups	torn mixed salad greens	2 L
	VINAIGRETTE	
2 tbsp	rice wine vinegar or white wine vinegar	25 mL
1 tbsp	liquid honey	15 mL
1/2 tsp	wasabi paste or dry mustard	2 mL
1/4 cup	vegetable oil	50 mL
1 tsp	chopped fresh chives	5 mL
1/4 tsp	each salt and pepper	1 mL

● VINAIGRETTE: In small bowl, whisk together vinegar, honey, wasabi paste and 1 tbsp (15 mL) water; gradually whisk in oil, chives, salt and pepper. *(Vinaigrette can be covered and refrigerated for up to 24 hours.)*

● In small bowl, combine cream cheese, chives, garlic, ginger, salt and pepper; spread over tortillas, leaving 1-inch (2.5 cm) border. Top with smoked salmon. Roll up tightly and place, seam side down, on cutting board.

● Divide salad greens among plates. Cut each tortilla roll into 1-inch (2.5 cm) thick slices, trimming ends. Arrange over lettuce. Drizzle with vinaigrette. Makes 4 servings.

Fresh Salmon Sandwiches with Herbs

Food writer Bonnie Stern takes the traditional salmon sandwich to new heights with freshly poached salmon and fresh herbs.

Per sandwich: about
- 340 calories
- 27 g protein
- 13 g fat
- 31 g carbohydrate
- good source of calcium and iron

1-1/2 lb	salmon fillets	750 g
1/4 cup	mayonnaise	50 mL
2 tbsp	plain yogurt or sour cream	25 mL
2 tbsp	lemon juice	25 mL
2 tbsp	each chopped fresh chives and parsley	25 mL
1 tbsp	chopped fresh tarragon (or 1/2 tsp/2 mL dried)	15 mL
2 tsp	Dijon mustard	10 mL
1/2 tsp	each salt and pepper	2 mL
16	slices black bread	16
1	bunch arugula (or 1 head curly endive), trimmed	1

● Place fillets in single layer in deep skillet of boiling water; reduce heat to medium and simmer gently for 6 minutes. Turn off heat. Let fillets stand in water for 5 minutes longer or until opaque and fish flakes easily when tested with fork. Drain and flake salmon into bowl, removing any bones.

● Combine mayonnaise, yogurt, lemon juice, chives, parsley, tarragon, mustard, salt and pepper; stir into salmon. Spread over 8 slices of the bread; top each with arugula. Sandwich with remaining bread. Makes 8 sandwiches.

TIP: You can substitute canned salmon for the fresh; use three 7-1/2 oz (213 mL) cans and omit salt.

CANNED CONVENIENCE

With cans of salmon and tuna in the pantry, it's easy to enjoy the goodness of fish more often.
Here's more than a week's worth of suggestions on how to use canned fish in delicious new ways and at a moment's notice.
These ideas work equally well with either tuna or salmon. For all recipes, use 6-1/2 oz (184 g) cans, drained.

Jazzed-Up Tuna Salad
● Combine 1 can tuna, flaked, with 1/4 cup (50 mL) each grated carrot and mayonnaise, 1 tbsp (15 mL) cocktail sauce and 2 tsp (10 mL) chopped fresh dill or basil. Use in tortillas or pita pockets or on bruschetta. Makes 2 servings.

Hot Tuna and Taters
● In small nonstick skillet, melt 2 tsp (10 mL) butter over medium-high heat; cook 1-1/2 cups (375 mL) frozen hash-browned potatoes, 2 tbsp (25 mL) grated onion and pinch pepper for 6 to 8 minutes or until golden. Sprinkle with 1 can chunk tuna, flaked. Pour in 2 eggs beaten with 2 tsp (10 mL) cold water and 1/4 cup (50 mL) shredded Swiss cheese. Cover and cook over medium heat for 4 minutes or until set. Sprinkle with diced sweet red pepper and chopped fresh parsley. Makes 2 servings.

Seaside Caesar
● Toss together 1 can chunk light tuna with 5 cups (1.25 L) torn romaine lettuce, 1/2 cup (125 mL) sliced mushrooms, 1/4 cup (50 mL) Caesar dressing and 2 tbsp (25 mL) grated Parmesan cheese. Makes 2 servings.

Tuna Chick-Pea Salad
● Toss together 1 can chunk light tuna, 1 can (19 oz/540 mL) chick-peas or kidney beans, drained, 3 plum tomatoes, chopped, 1 sweet yellow pepper, chopped, quarter of a cucumber, chopped, and 1/4 cup (50 mL) herb Italian dressing. Top with sliced green onions. Makes 4 servings.

Santa Fe Tuna Melt
● Spread 2 tbsp (25 mL) salsa on a pita bread. Top with quarter can of tuna and 1/4 cup (50 mL) shredded Monterey Jack cheese. Broil for 3 minutes or until cheese melts. Serve topped with avocado slices and squirt of lemon juice. Makes 1 serving.

Salmon and Green Bean Salad
● In saucepan, cook 8 oz (250 g) green beans in boiling water for 3 minutes; rinse in cold water and drain. Toss with 1 can salmon, broken into chunks. Place on bed of Bibb lettuce. Whisk together 2 tbsp (25 mL) sesame oil, 1 tbsp (15 mL) cider vinegar and pinch each granulated sugar, salt and pepper; drizzle over salad. Sprinkle with sesame seeds. Makes 2 servings.

Tuna Tomato Pasta
● In saucepan, simmer together 1 can (28 oz/796 mL) tomatoes, 2 cloves garlic, minced, and pinch hot pepper flakes until thickened, about 15 minutes. Stir in 1 can tuna, 2 green onions, sliced, and 1/2 cup (125 mL) pitted black olives. Serve over 12 oz (375 g) pasta, cooked. Makes 4 servings.

Suppertime Tuna Patties
● Stir together 1 cup (250 mL) mashed potatoes, 1 can tuna, 2 tsp (10 mL) each chopped fresh dill and lemon juice and 1 green onion, chopped. Shape into 4 patties; cook in greased nonstick skillet over medium heat for 5 minutes per side or until golden brown and crisp. Makes 4 servings.

Grilled Tuna Burgers

Fresh tuna burgers are a West Coast specialty. If fresh tuna is not available, substitute salmon fillets.

Per serving: about
- 516 calories
- 27 g fat
- very high source of fiber
- 34 g protein
- 37 g carbohydrate
- excellent source of iron

4	tuna fillets, 1/2 inch (1 cm) thick (about 1 lb/500 g)	4
1/4 cup	lemon juice	50 mL
2 tbsp	vegetable oil	25 mL
2 tbsp	soy sauce	25 mL
4	whole wheat buns, toasted	4
	SESAME DILL BUTTER	
1/4 cup	butter, softened	50 mL
1 tsp	toasted sesame seeds	5 mL
1 tsp	dried dillweed	5 mL
1 tsp	chopped green onion	5 mL
1 tsp	soy sauce	5 mL
1/2 tsp	sesame oil	2 mL
Pinch	pepper	Pinch

● SESAME DILL BUTTER: In small bowl, combine butter, sesame seeds, dill, onion, soy sauce, oil and pepper. *(Butter can be covered and refrigerated for up to 2 days.)*

● Arrange fillets in single layer in shallow dish. Combine lemon juice, oil and soy sauce; pour over fillets, turning to coat. Cover and let stand at room temperature for 30 minutes or refrigerate for up to 4 hours.

● Discarding marinade, place fillets on greased grill over medium-high heat; close lid and cook for about 5 minutes per side or until fish flakes easily when tested with fork.

● Spread each bun with 1 tbsp (15 mL) Sesame Dill Butter. Sandwich fillets in buns. Makes 4 servings.

TIP: Toast sesame seeds in skillet over medium heat, stirring, for 3 to 6 minutes or just until golden.

Crab Burgers with Avocado

Food writer Bonnie Stern transforms an everyday burger into a luxury treat for four lucky diners.

Per serving: about
- 595 calories
- 31 g fat
- excellent source of iron
- 33 g protein
- 47 g carbohydrate

1	large potato	1
1 lb	frozen crabmeat, thawed	500 g
3 tbsp	mayonnaise	50 mL
2	eggs	2
1 tsp	dry mustard	5 mL
1/2 tsp	each salt and pepper	2 mL
1/2 tsp	hot pepper sauce (optional)	2 mL
2 tbsp	vegetable oil	25 mL
1	ripe avocado	1
1 tbsp	lemon juice	15 mL
1	tomato	1
4	lettuce leaves	4
4	sesame seed hamburger buns	4

● Peel potato; cut into large chunks. In saucepan of boiling salted water, cook potato until tender. Drain well and mash.

● Meanwhile, squeeze crab dry; discard any bits of cartilage. To mashed potato, beat in mayonnaise, eggs, mustard, salt, pepper, and hot pepper sauce (if using); stir in crab. Shape into four 1-inch (2.5 cm) thick patties.

● In nonstick skillet, heat oil over medium heat; cook patties for 4 to 5 minutes per side or until browned and heated through.

● Meanwhile, peel and slice avocado thinly; sprinkle with lemon juice. Slice tomato thinly. Arrange lettuce on bottom halves of buns; top with patties, then avocado and tomato. Top with bun, pressing together gently. Makes 4 servings.

TIP: Two cans (each 7-1/2 oz/213 g) salmon or tuna can replace the crab.

Crunchy Lobster Rolls ▲

1	can (11.3 oz/320 g) frozen lobster meat, thawed	1
1 cup	chopped celery	250 mL
1/2 cup	chopped sweet red pepper	125 mL
1/3 cup	finely chopped onion	75 mL
2/3 cup	mayonnaise	150 mL
1/2 cup	sour cream	125 mL
2 tbsp	chopped fresh basil or dill	25 mL
1 tbsp	lemon juice	15 mL
Dash	hot pepper sauce	Dash
1	hard-cooked egg, chopped	1
	Salt and pepper	
8	oblong bread rolls, buttered	8
	Leaf lettuce	

● Drain lobster meat; squeeze dry and shred into small bowl. Add celery, red pepper and onion. *(Recipe can be prepared to this point, covered and refrigerated for up to 24 hours.)*

● In large bowl, stir together mayonnaise, sour cream, basil, lemon juice and hot pepper sauce; stir in egg and lobster mixture, tossing to combine. Season with salt and pepper to taste. Line rolls with lettuce; divide lobster mixture among rolls. Makes 8 servings.

N*o trip to Atlantic Canada is complete without a lobster roll — chunks of local lobster, crunchy with celery and nestled in a soft bun. We've taken a few liberties with fresh herbs, but you get the picture.*

Per serving: about
• 394 calories • 14 g protein
• 24 g fat • 30 g carbohydrate

TIP: Three pounds (1.5 kg) of lobster, cooked, cooled and picked over, will yield the 2 cups (500 mL) meat necessary for this recipe.

Scallop Salad ◀

8 oz	asparagus, trimmed	250 g
8 oz	bay scallops	250 g
Half	small red onion	Half
1	orange	1
1	small head Boston lettuce	1
	DRESSING	
2 tbsp	orange juice	25 mL
1-1/2 tsp	grated lime or lemon rind	7 mL
1 tbsp	lime or lemon juice	15 mL
1 tbsp	rice vinegar or cider vinegar	15 mL
1 tbsp	vegetable oil	15 mL
1 tsp	liquid honey	5 mL
1/4 tsp	salt	1 mL
1 tbsp	each chopped fresh parsley and mint	15 mL

● In steamer, steam asparagus for 4 minutes or just until tender-crisp. Rinse under cold water; drain well.

● In saucepan, cover scallops with cold water; bring to boil. Reduce heat and simmer for about 1 minute or just until opaque in center. Drain and rinse under cold water; drain again.

● Slice half of the onion into rings; chop remaining half finely. Set aside. Peel orange, removing outside membrane. Slice into rounds; halve. In large bowl, combine asparagus, scallops, onion rings and orange slices.

● DRESSING: In small bowl, whisk together orange juice, lime rind and juice, vinegar, oil, honey and salt; stir in parsley, mint and reserved chopped onion. Pour over scallop mixture. Reserving dressing, arrange scallop mixture on lettuce-lined plates. Drizzle with dressing. Makes 2 servings.

If you can't find the small bay scallops, cut sea scallops into quarters.

Per serving: about
- 270 calories
- 8 g fat
- high source of fiber
- 24 g protein
- 28 g carbohydrate

Potato Salad with Shrimp

1 lb	small red potatoes (about 6), unpeeled	500 g
1/2 cup	chopped celery	125 mL
1/4 cup	chopped red onion	50 mL
2 tbsp	chopped fresh parsley	25 mL
1	hard-cooked egg	1
6 oz	cooked peeled shrimp	175 g
	DRESSING	
1/4 cup	ricotta cheese	50 mL
2 tbsp	freshly grated Parmesan cheese	25 mL
1/4 cup	milk	50 mL
1 tbsp	olive oil	15 mL
1 tbsp	white wine vinegar	15 mL
1 tsp	Dijon mustard	5 mL
1/4 tsp	salt	1 mL
Pinch	pepper	Pinch
1	clove garlic, minced	1

● DRESSING: In blender, combine ricotta and Parmesan cheeses, milk, oil, vinegar, mustard, salt and pepper; blend until smooth. Stir in garlic.

● In saucepan of boiling salted water, cook potatoes for 20 minutes or just until tender. Drain and cut into bite-size chunks.

● In bowl, combine potatoes, celery, onion and parsley; add dressing and toss to coat. *(Salad can be prepared to this point, covered and refrigerated for up to 24 hours.)* Slice egg; arrange over salad along with shrimp. Makes 4 servings.

Enjoy this hearty summer salad in season, or whenever you feel like a bit of summer.

Per serving: about
- 250 calories
- 9 g fat
- good source of iron
- 19 g protein
- 23 g carbohydrate

Salmon on Rice and Beans

Serve a wedge of orange or lemon alongside the salmon so you can squeeze it over the hot fish. It adds a great appetite-whetting whiff of citrus and freshens the fish.

Per serving: about
- 605 calories
- 21 g fat
- very high source of fiber
- 33 g protein
- 70 g carbohydrate
- good source of iron

1 lb	salmon fillet (with skin)	500 g
Pinch	salt	Pinch
1 cup	parboiled rice	250 mL
Pinch	dried thyme	Pinch
1	can (19 oz/540 mL) red kidney beans, drained and rinsed	1
1	small mango, peach or nectarine, peeled and diced	1
	Lettuce leaves	
	DRESSING	
1 tsp	coarsely grated orange rind	5 mL
1/2 cup	orange juice	125 mL
1/4 cup	vegetable oil	50 mL
3 tbsp	lime or lemon juice	50 mL
2	large green onions, chopped	2
2	cloves garlic, minced	2
3/4 tsp	curry powder	4 mL
1/2 tsp	each salt, pepper, dried thyme and hot pepper sauce	2 mL

● DRESSING: In small bowl, whisk together orange rind and juice, oil, lime juice, onions, garlic, curry powder, salt, pepper, thyme and hot pepper sauce.

● Cut salmon crosswise into 2-inch (5 cm) wide strips. Place in glass dish just big enough to hold strips in single layer. Remove 2 tbsp (25 mL) of the dressing; brush over fish. Let stand for 30 minutes at room temperature.

● Meanwhile, in saucepan, bring 2 cups (500 mL) water and salt to boil; add rice and thyme. Reduce heat to low, cover and cook for about 20 minutes or until rice is tender and water is absorbed; fluff with fork. Pour in all but 1 tbsp (15 mL) of the dressing; add beans and mango and toss gently with fork to combine.

● Place salmon, skin side down, on greased grill over medium-high heat; close lid and cook, without turning, for 7 to 10 minutes or until fish flakes easily when tested with fork.

● Line plates with lettuce; mound rice mixture on top. Using metal spatula, carefully lift salmon off skin; place on top of rice. Drizzle with remaining dressing. Makes 4 servings.

Tuna Salad in Tomatoes

When the cupboard is almost bare, reliable canned tuna can rescue the supper situation. Here's one fresh and healthful way to use it.

Per serving: about
- 155 calories
- 4 g fat
- good source of iron
- 17 g protein
- 15 g carbohydrate

1	can (6-1/2 oz/184 g) water-packed tuna, drained and flaked	1	2 tsp	lemon juice	10 mL
				Pepper	
2	green onions, chopped	2	3	tomatoes	3
1	stalk celery, diced	1			
1/2 cup	corn kernels	125 mL			
2 tbsp	each chopped fresh coriander and parsley	25 mL			
2 tbsp	light mayonnaise	25 mL			
2 tbsp	low-fat plain yogurt	25 mL			

● In bowl, combine tuna, onions, celery, corn, coriander, parsley, mayonnaise, yogurt, lemon juice, and pepper to taste.

● Quarter tomatoes, cutting almost through; spoon tuna mixture into center. Makes 3 servings.

TIP: Explore other herbs if they are more available than coriander. Dill or basil is a tasty substitute, and if you have only parsley, just add more of it.

Marinated Herring Salad

1	jar (200 g) marinated herring, drained	1
1 cup	diced cooked potatoes	250 mL
1 cup	diced cooked beets	250 mL
2	apples, chopped	2
1/2 cup	chopped dill pickles	125 mL
Half	small Spanish onion, sliced	Half
8	lettuce leaves	8
3	hard-cooked eggs, quartered	3

CREAM DRESSING		
1 cup	whipping cream	250 mL
1 tbsp	white vinegar	15 mL
1 tsp	prepared mustard	5 mL
1/2 tsp	dried dillweed	2 mL
1/4 tsp	each salt and pepper	1 mL

● CREAM DRESSING: In small bowl, whisk together cream, vinegar, mustard, dill, salt and pepper.

● In large bowl, combine herring, potatoes, beets, apples, pickles and onion; add dressing and toss lightly. Arrange on lettuce-lined plates. Garnish with eggs. Makes 8 servings.

This Dutch salad originated in Nova Scotia with the Mutsaers family. It's an excellent introduction to herring for anyone who has not yet had the thrill of their first taste.

Per serving: about
- 203 calories
- 5 g protein
- 14 g fat
- 16 g carbohydrate

Warm Fillet Salad ▼

4 tsp	white wine vinegar	20 mL
1	clove garlic, minced	1
1	green onion, chopped	1
1/2 tsp	salt	2 mL
1/4 tsp	pepper	1 mL
1/4 cup	olive oil	50 mL
1 cup	diced tomato	250 mL
2 tbsp	diced sweet green pepper	25 mL
2 tbsp	chopped fresh parsley	25 mL
2 tbsp	chopped fresh coriander (or extra parsley)	25 mL
1 lb	fish fillets	500 g
	Vegetable oil	
4 cups	chopped lettuce	1 L

● In bowl, whisk together vinegar, garlic, onion, salt and pepper; gradually whisk in oil. Add tomato, green pepper, parsley and coriander; set vinaigrette aside.

● Place fillets on greased baking sheet; brush lightly with oil. Broil for about 5 minutes or until fish flakes easily when tested with fork. Arrange on lettuce-lined plates; spoon vinaigrette over top. Makes 4 servings.

Coriander, also known as cilantro, adds a fresh note to a very quick fish salad supper.

Per serving: about
- 245 calories
- 23 g protein
- 15 g fat
- 4 g carbohydrate
- good source of iron

Spiced Shrimp ◀

1 tsp	each paprika and ground cumin	5 mL
1 tsp	packed brown sugar	5 mL
1/2 tsp	each salt, dry mustard and oregano	2 mL
Pinch	each chili powder and cayenne pepper	Pinch
1 lb	extra-large peeled shrimp (raw or cooked)	500 g
1 tbsp	vegetable oil	15 mL
	Lime wedges (optional)	

● In small bowl, combine paprika, cumin, sugar, salt, mustard, oregano, chili powder and cayenne; sprinkle over shrimp in large bowl and toss to coat evenly. *(Shrimp can be covered and refrigerated for up to 3 hours.)*

● In nonstick skillet, heat oil over medium-high heat; stir-fry shrimp until cooked through and no longer opaque, 3 to 4 minutes for raw, 2 to 3 minutes for cooked. Serve hot with lime (if using). Makes about 40 pieces.

If your entertaining menus are big on shrimp, you'll enjoy serving these hot appetizers. But be warned — guests are sure to waylay the serving platter every time it passes by!

Per piece: about
• 17 calories   • 2 g protein
• trace fat and carbohydrate

Matane Shrimp with Garlic Butter

1/4 cup	butter, softened	50 mL
1-1/2 tsp	dry white wine or lemon juice	7 mL
3 tbsp	minced fresh parsley	50 mL
2	cloves garlic, minced	2
1 lb	raw shrimp, peeled and deveined	500 g
	Salt and pepper	

● In bowl, beat together butter, wine, parsley and garlic. Place on plastic wrap; using wrap, form into log shape. Refrigerate for up to 2 days.

● In large skillet, heat 3 tbsp (50 mL) of the garlic butter over medium-high heat until foam subsides; sauté shrimp, tossing often, for about 4 minutes or until firm and pink. Season with salt and pepper to taste. Serve topped with remaining garlic butter. Makes 4 appetizers.

Choice pink shrimp from Quebec go Gallic with garlic. If you like garlicky butter on snails, you'll love what it does for shrimp.

Per serving: about
• 195 calories   • 18 g protein
• 13 g fat   • 1 g carbohydrate

Shrimp Quesadillas

1 cup	shredded skim or part-skim mozzarella cheese	250 mL
8	8-inch (20 cm) flour tortillas	8
1/2 cup	diced tomato	125 mL
1/2 cup	cooked salad shrimp (2 oz/60 g)	125 mL
1/2 cup	crumbled feta or firm goat cheese (chèvre)	125 mL
1/3 cup	chopped fresh dill	75 mL
1/4 cup	chopped red or green onion	50 mL
1/4 tsp	hot pepper sauce	1 mL

● Sprinkle half of the mozzarella cheese evenly over half of each tortilla. In small bowl, stir together tomato, shrimp, feta cheese, dill, onion and hot pepper sauce; spoon over mozzarella. Top with remaining mozzarella. Fold plain half over top, pressing edges together.

● In large nonstick skillet over medium-high heat, cook 2 quesadillas at a time for 3 to 5 minutes or until lightly browned. Turn and cook until cheese is melted and bottom is lightly browned. Cut each into 3 wedges. Makes 24 pieces.

Quesadillas are a trendy appetizer — and a wonderful way to stretch shrimp for a party. Use a pizza cutter or long chef's knife to cut quesadillas.

Per piece: about
• 70 calories   • 4 g protein
• 2 g fat   • 9 g carbohydrate

Appetizer Mussels ▲

Sitting around a bowl of mussels, dipping them into their white-wine cooking liquid or into melted garlic butter, is a grand way to start a summer party on Prince Edward Island.

Per serving: about
- 50 calories
- 1 g fat
- 4 g protein
- 2 g carbohydrate

2 lb	mussels	1 kg
1 cup	dry white wine	250 mL
1/2 cup	finely chopped celery	125 mL
2	green onions, chopped	2
1/4 tsp	pepper	1 mL
Pinch	salt	Pinch
1/4 cup	each chopped fresh parsley and chives	50 mL

● Scrub mussels, removing any beards. Discard any mussels that do not close when tapped.

● In large saucepan, bring wine, celery, onions, pepper and salt to simmer. Add mussels; cover and bring just to boil. Cook for about 6 minutes or until mussels open. Discard any that do not open. Sprinkle with parsley and chives.

● With slotted spoon, transfer to large warmed bowl. Pour cooking liquid into separate bowl for dipping. Makes 8 appetizers.

Clam Fritters

2	cans (each 5 oz/142 g) baby clams	2
1	egg	1
1/3 cup	milk	75 mL
1/4 tsp	each salt and pepper	1 mL
3/4 cup	all-purpose flour	175 mL
3/4 tsp	baking powder	4 mL
	Vegetable oil for deep-frying	

● Drain clams, reserving 3 tbsp (50 mL) clam juice in bowl. Add egg, milk, salt and pepper; stir in clams.

● Stir together flour and baking powder; add all at once to clam mixture, stirring until blended.

● In deep-fryer, heat 2 inches (5 cm) of oil to 340°F (175°C) or until 1-inch (2.5 cm) cube of white bread turns golden brown in 70 seconds.

● In batches, drop tablespoonfuls (15 mL) of batter into hot oil; deep-fry for about 5 minutes, turning halfway through, or until deep golden brown. Drain fritters on paper towels. Keep warm on baking sheet in 250°F (120°C) oven. Serve immediately. Makes about 26 pieces.

Locally gathered fresh and home-dried clams have always been a major food source for the northwest native bands, from which this recipe originates. Serve simply with a squeeze of lemon or a dipping bowl of tartar sauce.

Per piece: about
- 42 calories
- 2 g fat
- 2 g protein
- 3 g carbohydrate

TIP: Fans of hot food may want to spike the batter with a dash of hot pepper sauce.

Smoked Salmon Japanese-Style

8	thin slices smoked salmon (about 6 oz/175 g)	8
2	leaves Belgian endive	2
1 tbsp	Japanese rice vinegar	15 mL
1 tbsp	extra virgin olive oil	15 mL
	Pepper	
1 tsp	finely slivered pickled ginger	5 mL
	Watercress (optional)	

● Arrange salmon on chilled salad plates. Cut endive lengthwise into very thin strips. Scatter over salmon.

● Combine vinegar with oil; drizzle over salmon. Sprinkle with pepper to taste. Sprinkle with ginger; garnish with watercress (if using). Makes 4 appetizers.

Rice vinegar and slivered pickled ginger (beni shoga) are available in Japanese groceries and some supermarkets.

Per serving: about
- 89 calories
- 5 g fat
- 8 g protein
- 2 g carbohydrate

Grilled Sardines

8 oz	sardines or smelts	250 g
2 tsp	olive oil	10 mL
	Salt and pepper	
	Balsamic vinegar	

● Using small sharp knife, slit underside of fish from tail to jaw. Clean and rinse; cut off head if desired. Pat fish dry. Brush with oil; sprinkle with pinch each salt and pepper.

● Place fish in grilling basket and place on grill over medium-high heat; close lid and cook, turning once, for 12 to 15 minutes or until skin is golden brown and crisp. Sprinkle with vinegar, salt and pepper to taste. Makes 4 appetizers.

Portuguese-style grilled sardines or smelts, or other small fish, are downright irresistible.

Per serving: about
- 70 calories
- 4 g fat
- 9 g protein
- 0 g carbohydrate

Oysters on the Half Shell ▶

An oyster bar is a relaxing way to entertain.

Per serving: about
- 60 calories
- 6 g protein
- 2 g fat
- 4 g carbohydrate
- excellent source of iron

36	oysters	36
6	lemon wedges	6
	Large sprigs parsley	
	Pepper	

- Make bed of crushed ice on 6 deep plates and place in freezer.

- Shuck oysters, retaining as much liquor as possible in cupped bottom shell. Discard flat upper shell. Balance oysters in bottom shell on bed of ice.

- Garnish each plate with lemon wedge and parsley. Season with pepper to taste. Makes 6 appetizers.

Whitefish Caviar Spread

For extra-special occasions, top this easy yet elegant spread with a second jar of whitefish caviar. Guests will know you love them! Serve with crackers, cucumber slices or Belgian endive.

Per tbsp (15 mL): about
- 35 calories
- 1 g protein
- 3 g fat
- 1 g carbohydrate

1	pkg (8 oz/250 g) cream cheese, softened	1
1 cup	sour cream	250 mL
1 tsp	lemon juice	5 mL
1/4 tsp	hot pepper sauce	1 mL
1	pkg unflavored gelatin	1
1/2 cup	dry white wine	125 mL
1 tbsp	chopped fresh chives or green onion	15 mL
1 tsp	chopped fresh dill	5 mL
1	jar (1.75 oz/50 g) whitefish caviar	1
	Dill sprigs	
	Lemon slices	

- In bowl, beat together cream cheese, sour cream, lemon juice and hot pepper sauce until smooth.

- In small saucepan or microwaveable bowl, sprinkle gelatin over wine; let stand for 1 minute. Warm over low heat or in microwave, stirring until gelatin dissolves; blend into cream cheese mixture along with chives, chopped dill and caviar.

- Spoon into serving bowl, smoothing top. Refrigerate for at least 4 hours or until firm or for up to 2 days. Garnish with dill sprigs and lemon. Makes 2-1/2 cups (625 mL).

Creamy Shrimp Dip

Surround *a bowlful of this popular dip with carrots, sliced fennel, celery, radishes, cucumber and breadsticks. Then relax and watch the guests buzz back and forth to the bowl.*

Per tbsp (15 mL): about
- 30 calories
- 4 g protein
- 2 g fat
- trace carbohydrate

6 oz	cooked salad shrimp (about 1 cup/250 mL)	175 g
3 oz	light cream cheese, softened	90 g
1/4 cup	finely chopped onion	50 mL
1 tbsp	lemon juice	15 mL
2 tsp	chopped fresh dill (or 1 tsp/5 mL dried dillweed)	10 mL
1-1/2 tsp	horseradish	7 mL
1/4 tsp	Worcestershire sauce	1 mL
Dash	hot pepper sauce	Dash
Pinch	each salt and pepper	Pinch
	Fresh dill sprig	

● Set aside 2 of the shrimp. In food processor, blend together remaining shrimp, cream cheese, onion, lemon juice, dill, horseradish, Worcestershire sauce, hot pepper sauce, salt and pepper until almost smooth.

● Transfer to small serving bowl; cover and refrigerate for at least 1 hour or for up to 12 hours. Just before serving, stir and garnish with reserved shrimp and dill sprig. Makes 1 cup (250 mL).

Maritime Crab Dip

Warm seafood dips are a favorite in Atlantic Canada. Try scooping up this one with crackers, pita wedges or crudités. Leftovers make a grand topping for baked potatoes.

Per tbsp (15 mL): about
- 36 calories
- 1 g protein
- 3 g fat
- 1 g carbohydrate

1	pkg (4 oz/125 g) cream cheese, softened	1
1/4 cup	mayonnaise	50 mL
3 tbsp	chili sauce	50 mL
1 tsp	chopped fresh parsley	5 mL
1/2 tsp	pepper	2 mL
1/2 tsp	Dijon mustard	2 mL
2	cans (each 6 oz/170 g) crabmeat, drained	2
1	green onion, chopped	1
1/2 cup	fresh bread crumbs	125 mL
2 tbsp	butter, melted	25 mL

● In bowl, beat cream cheese with mayonnaise until smooth; beat in chili sauce, parsley, pepper and mustard. Stir in crabmeat and onion; spoon into greased 2-cup (500 mL) ovenproof dish.

● In small bowl, stir bread crumbs with butter until moistened; sprinkle over crab mixture. Bake in 325°F (160°C) oven for 20 minutes or until heated through. Broil for 1 minute or until crumbs are golden brown. Makes 1-3/4 cups (425 mL).

Lobster Dip

Melted *butter and lemon are classics with lobster, but when Prince Edward Island restaurateur Dot Toombs cooks lobster, she serves this sweet and tangy dipping sauce.*

Per tbsp (15 mL): about
- 90 calories
- 1 g protein
- 6 g fat
- 8 g carbohydrate

1/2 cup	granulated sugar	125 mL
4 tsp	all-purpose flour	20 mL
3/4 tsp	dry mustard	4 mL
1/3 cup	milk	75 mL
1/4 cup	white vinegar	50 mL
1	egg yolk	1
2 tsp	butter	10 mL
2/3 cup	Miracle Whip salad dressing	150 mL

● In heavy saucepan, whisk together sugar, flour and mustard; whisk in milk, vinegar and egg yolk. Cook over medium heat, stirring constantly, for about 4 minutes or until boiling. Boil for 1 minute. Remove from heat; stir in butter until melted.

● Pour into bowl; place plastic wrap directly on surface and refrigerate for about 2 hours or until cool. Stir in salad dressing. Makes 1 cup (250 mL).

Crowd-Pleasing Crab Cakes ▲

2	eggs	2
2 tbsp	mayonnaise	25 mL
1-1/2 tsp	horseradish	7 mL
1/4 tsp	each pepper and hot pepper sauce	1 mL
Pinch	salt	Pinch
8 oz	crabmeat	250 g
1/4 cup	minced green onions	50 mL
1/2 cup	cracker crumbs	125 mL
1/4 cup	vegetable oil	50 mL

● In large bowl, beat eggs lightly; mix in mayonnaise, horseradish, pepper, hot pepper sauce and salt. Add crabmeat, onions and half of the cracker crumbs; mix well with fork.

● With wet hands, form into 6 large or 12 small 3/4-inch (2 cm) thick patties; press into remaining crumbs to coat both sides.

● In large skillet, heat half of the oil over medium heat; cook half of the crab cakes for 2 to 3 minutes per side or until crisp and golden brown. Repeat with remaining crab cakes. Makes 6 servings.

J*ust watch the party crowd form around a plate of these crab cakes. If using frozen crabmeat, drain it in sieve, pressing out liquid.*

Per serving: about
- 213 calories
- 16 g fat
- 12 g protein
- 5 g carbohydrate

The Contributors

For your easy reference, we have included an alphabetical listing of recipes by contributor.

Jeffrey Alford and Naomi Duguid
Shrimp and Rice Soup, 71

Carla Azevedo
Clams in Coriander Sauce, 68

Elizabeth Baird
Appetizer Mussels, 84
Baked Stuffed Whitefish, 31
Chili-Crusted Salmon
    Steaks, 36
Clam Lasagna Roll-Ups, 50
Easy Salmon Chowder, 63
Fish Cakes, 19
Haddock with Light Cream
    Sauce, 15
Lemon Pepper Roasted Cod, 27
Lobster Dip, 88
Matane Shrimp with Garlic
    Butter, 83
Pan-Fried Fillets with
    Mushrooms, 20
Pickerel Waves, 42
Pizza-Style Fish Fillets, 27
Roasted Salmon with Wild
    Rice, 30
Salmon on Rice and Beans, 80
Sauced Smoked Fish, 31
Shrimp Sausage Gumbo, 10
Smoked Salmon
    Japanese-Style, 85
Smoked Salmon Strata, 53
Steamed Fillets with Herb
    Vinaigrette, 17
Tomato Mussel Chowder, 67
Warm Fillet Salad, 81
Whitefish Caviar Spread, 86

Suzanne Bourret
Cedar-Planked Salmon, 39

Pam Collacott
Mussel Soup Italiano, 66

Judith Comfort
Marinated Herring Salad, 81
Maritime Lobster Chowder, 64

Brenda Creighton
Lobster Quiche, 48

Elaine Elliot and Virginia Lee
Haddock with Peach and
    Pepper Salsa, 21

Nancy Enright
Baked Salmon-Stuffed
    Potatoes, 53

Carol Ferguson
Easy Cioppino, 67
Linguine with Clams and
    Tomatoes, 59
Potato Salad with Shrimp, 79
Scallop Salad, 79

Margaret Fraser
Smoke-Grilled Salmon, 34
Tomato Dill Trout, 14
Tuna Fisherman's Pie, 52

Joanne Good
Chili Cheese Fish Stacks, 24

Jurgen Gothe
Smoked Salmon Rolls on
    Mixed Greens, 74

Heather Howe
Shrimp Pasta Bake, 55

Anne Lindsay
Barbecued Red Snapper, 41
Barbecued Trout with Light
    Tartar Sauce, 44
Chicken and Shrimp
    Jambalaya, 54
Grilled Tuna Burger, 76
Halibut Steaks with
    Tomato-Basil Sauce, 45
Linguine with Scallops and
    Spinach, 60
Shrimp in Black Bean Sauce, 9
Spiced Shrimp, 83
Tuna Salad in Tomatoes, 80
Shrimp Quesadillas, 83

Sondra Mawdsley
Mom's Best Qualicum
    Chowder, 64

Rose Murray
Asian Grilled Salmon, 38
Baked Stuffed Whitefish, 31

Busy-Night Lemon-Baked
    Fish, 25
Chili-Crusted Salmon
    Steaks, 36
Corn and Smoked Salmon
    Chowder, 63
Creamy Shrimp Dip, 88
Oysters on the Half Shell, 86
Parmesan Baked Fillets, 25
Peanut Crunch Fillets, 26
Quick Curried Fillets, 18
Risotto from the Sea, 10
Salmon on Rice and Beans, 80
Sauced Smoked Fish, 31
Smoked Salmon Strata, 53

Daphna Rabinovitch
Smoked Salmon and Chèvre
    Quiche, 49

Marsha Rosen
Lean Fish with Salsa, 13

Bertha Skye
Crispy-Fried Pickerel, 20

Linda Stephen
Grouper in Coconut Curry
    Sauce, 68
Tuna with Papaya Salad, 45

Bonnie Stern
Arctic Char with Shrimp, 27
Crab Burgers with
    Avocado, 76
Fresh Salmon Sandwiches
    with Herbs, 74
Roasted Salmon with
    Tomatoes and Lentils, 32
Singapore Shrimp Noodles, 60
Swordfish and Olive
    Mayonnaise Sandwich, 72

Anita Stewart
Clam Fritters, 85
Tomato-Smothered
    Halibut, 32

Ann Teeters
Mediterranean-Style Tuna, 61

Stephen Wong
Steamed Whole Rockfish, 16

Photography Credits

LAURA ARSIE: cover
photograph of Elizabeth Baird;
photograph of the Canadian
Living Test Kitchen staff.

FRED BIRD: pages 19, 24, 26,
29, 51, 54, 77, 81.

DOUGLAS BRADSHAW:
pages 4, 7, 11, 57, 58, 78.

CHRISTOPHER CAMPBELL:
pages 38, 89.

PETER CHOU: pages 36, 43.

MARINA DODIS: page 16.

YVONNE DUIVENVOORDEN:
pages 40, 65, 70, 75.

ANDRÉ GALLANT: page 84.

FRANK GRANT: pages 66, 69.

MICHAEL MAHOVLICH:
page 8.

VINCENT NOGUCHI:
pages 14, 23, 33, 61.

ROBERT WIGINGTON: front
cover; pages 13, 35, 47, 62, 73,
82, 87.

In the Canadian Living Test Kitchen. Clockwise from left: Elizabeth Baird (food director), Heather Howe (manager), Susan Van Hezewijk, Emily Richards, Donna Bartolini (associate food director), Daphna Rabinovitch (associate food director) and Jennifer MacKenzie.

Special Thanks

Praise and thanks go to the talented and enthusiastic team who put together *Canadian Living's Best Fish and Seafood*. First, to the Canadian Living Test Kitchen staff — home economists Emily Richards, Susan Van Hezewijk, Jennifer MacKenzie and manager Heather Howe — and to associate food directors Daphna Rabinovitch and Donna Bartolini for their leadership role in testing and creating recipes to appear in *Canadian Living* and in all of the cookbooks. Appreciation goes also to our valued food writers (noted above), managing editor Susan Antonacci, editorial assistant Olga Goncalves, senior editor Julia Armstrong, our copy department under Michael Killingsworth and our art department guided by Cate Cochran. Special thanks to our meticulous senior food editor, Beverley Renahan, for her high standards of consistency and accuracy and to editor-in-chief Bonnie Cowan and publisher Caren King for their support.

There are others to thank, too. On the visual side — our photographers (noted above); prop stylists Maggi Jones, Janet Walkinshaw, Shelly Tauber, Bridget Sargeant and Susan Doherty-Hannaford who provide the backgrounds, dishes and embellishments for the luscious food photos; and food stylists Kate Bush, Ruth

Gangbar, Debby Charendoff Moses, Lucie Richard, Olga Truchan, Jennifer McLagan, Jill Snider, Sharon Dale and Kathy Robertson who do the creative cooking, arranging and garnishing of recipes.

Book designers Gord Sibley and Dale Vokey are responsible for the splendid new design of the *Best* Series. Thanks also to Albert Cummings, president of Madison Press Books.

Working with Wanda Nowakowska, associate editorial director at Madison, is always a pleasure — certainly for her high standard of workmanship and creativity that have made the whole *Best* series so user-friendly and attractive, but also for her calm and always thoughtful, kind and generous nature. Thanks also to Tina Gaudino, Donna Chong, Rosemary Hillary and others at Madison Press Books.

Appreciation for their contribution at Random House is extended to Duncan Shields (mass marketing sales manager), Mary Jane Boreham, members of the marketing and publicity departments — Kathleen Bain, Pat Cairns, Sheila Kay, Cathy Paine, Maria Medeiros and Deborah Bjorgan — and to president and publisher David Kent.

Elizabeth Baird

Index

Grilled, roasted or chowdered — fish has never tasted this good!

**CANADIAN LIVING
TESTED TILL PERFECT
KITCHEN**

Trust Canadian Living to bring you the BEST!